D. L. Moody

D. L. Moody

Faith Coxe Bailey

MOODY PRESS
CHICAGO

Original title D. L. Moody;
The Valley and the World

ISBN 0-8024-0039-6

35 37 39 40 38 36 34

Printed in the United States of America

Chapter One

"YOU COME BACK HERE, Dwight Moody! What in the world do you mean? Set me to work —and then just walk off!" Young D.L. Moody turned and saw his brother George drop his ax to the ground. George sputtered again, "You can't get away with it. You set me to work like I was a hired hand. Then you stand around and—."

"And organize," D.L. said, grinning.

"Organize! Huh—another word for pushing work off on another fellow. I heard you talk before, Dwight. You grab that ax and start chopping."

In another moment, his big brother would start after him. But it was too nice a day for a real squabble. So D.L. walked toward the woodpile, reluctantly. "One's enough for this job," he started to explain. "You follow my system, George, and you—."

"Chop!" George said.

For the next few moments there was no sound in the back yard of the Massachusetts farmhouse but the steady thud of ax on wood and the instantaneous splitting of pine. Overhead a bluejay rasped, and D.L. thought in irritation that the bird was mocking his sweat. When the jay scratched out a last remark, curving away over the trees, D.L. hated the bird for flaunting its freedom. He lifted his ax more slowly, slamming it down with force but no bounce.

"Chop wood in the fall," he grunted, half to his brother, more to himself. "Hoe corn in the spring. Pick beans in the summer. That ain't no life."

George straightened up, pulling the sweat from

his forehead with the back of his hand. "Why don't you organize something better?"

"Sick and tired of being squeezed into this valley." Now the ax swung fiercely. "Sick and tired." Up with the ax. "Sick and—," down with the ax, fiercely, "—tired."

"You got growing pains. You're but sixteen, Dwight. I had 'em too."

D.L. rested his ax, leaning on the handle. "These growin' pains are gonna grow me right off this farm and out of this valley and over them hills."

"You're too big for your breeches, Dwight."

He flung down his ax. "Then I'll get me new breeches. Fancy ones. City ones. Not wood-chopping breeches." A chunk of pine splintered off from George's ax and hit him sharply against the shins. He sidestepped but he didn't look down. Instead, he studied the low hills in the distance, as brown against the sky as the turkey gravy his mother was sure to serve at dinner. Crossly he flung the thoughts of his mother and the family's Thanksgiving dinner out of his mind. "A man is only so much muscles and blood and brains," he told his brother. "It's up to him what he makes out of that raw stuff. Well, I'm gonna make something, something big. You wait and see."

It was Thanksgiving Day, 1853. Later at the table, young D.L. hunched up his shoulders, ducked his head and, protecting his plate with a curved arm, gave his full attention to the turkey, mashed potatoes, and squash. When he had almost come to the end of his second plateful, be began to listen to the conversation between his mother and his Uncle Samuel, up from his Boston shoestore for the holiday.

"He comes up and stuffs himself fat on our victuals," he thought as his uncle belched behind his napkin. "Then he goes back to the big city, shaking the dust of the road in our faces and thinking us all poor country relatives." The rings on his uncle's hands glittered. If only *he* could get to that city on the other side of the hills, he could get rich too.

Uncle Samuel patted his mouth politely and belched again. "I declare, Betsy Holton Moody, this pie of yours is richer'n Beacon Hill."

D.L. leaned down the table. "Uncle Samuel, them folks on Beacon Hill—," he began.

But his mother rapped the table. "Dwight, your uncle's plate. Pass it like a good boy."

D.L. paid no attention. "They're all rolling in money, huh?"

"Dwight! Your uncle wants another piece of pie."

He handed down the plate and kept on talking. "I'm figuring on being rich some day, Uncle Samuel."

His mother drew in her breath, but his uncle beamed and nodded. "That's a good ambition. It's a free country, Dwight."

"I'm figuring on coming down to Boston."

"Dwight." His mother's cheeks were getting pink, a sure sign of trouble ahead.

But Uncle Samuel clucked pleasantly. "Now, Betsy, dreaming never hurt nobody."

So D. L. persisted. "Right away."

"What's that!"

The prongs of D. L.'s fork drew a wild circle in mid-air. "Figure you need a new hand to help out with winter trade."

His uncle's chair scraped the wood floor. "Why, Dwight, boy, I'd be happier than a clam at high tide to oblige you, but it just so happens—."

"I don't aim to work for you long," D.L. hurried on. "Just till I get my bearings and decide what I really want." His uncle said nothing. The chair squeaked back and forth. Elatedly, D.L. thought, it must be settled. Easier than he'd hoped!

Suddenly, across the table, George's chin jutted out. "You hire old Dwight here, and he'll be running your store before you know it."

D.L.'s chair shot back, and he grabbed for his brother. But George was halfway out of the room, his pie in his hand. From the doorway, he taunted, "Watch out, Uncle Samuel. You watch out for old Dwight. He'll run the store right out from under you."

D.L. let him go, concentrating on his uncle. "Strike a bargain, Uncle Samuel. I'll go back to Boston with you tomorrow." His uncle had to see he could not stay there on the farm, chopping wood for the rest of his life. "You can hire me for less wages'n you pay anybody else. That's a bargain."

His uncle said nothing as he pushed his chair back from the table, giving his napkin and his lap a little shake that spilled crumbs of turkey and stuffing to the floor. He belched. "I'm fuller'n a healthy hog, Betsy," he said ponderously. Then he turned to D.L. "Settle down there, boy. I never struck no bargain. I reckon you'll call me mean as goose grease, but the truth is there's no place in my Boston shoestore for you. You stay put right here in this valley and look after your widow mother."

But D.L. had caught hold of an idea and he was not going to be pried loose. Uncle Samuel could help him escape from the valley, and there was no reason why he should not. But later, when he faced his uncle out by the woodpile, his uncle made his reasons very plain. "What about your mamma, Dwight? You got some obligation to Betsy, after all. The way she's brought up all of you. Why, you were but a four-year-old tyke when your papa died."

8

"I'd send money home," D.L. murmured.

As his uncle fiddled with his waistcoat buttons, his rings sparkled in the fall sun. D.L. could not take his eyes from them. "'Tisn't just your mamma, Dwight, that makes me say no. 'Tisn't just the way I feel about a country boy knowing his place and staying there. But, Dwight—." His uncle puffed out his cheeks. "Dwight, you're a hotheaded, unlearned young fool. You're wild. Who pinned up the notice for the temperance meeting last month?"

"But—."

"Gathered up a crowd of hard-working farmers to hear the lecture and there wasn't no lecture at all."

"Can't a fellow have some fun?"

"Fun and tomfoolery—that's what your wildness is in the country. But the city's different. A hundred ways for a young fellow to go wrong. Especially one that's got a wild streak in his nature. He'd get out of hand. Disgrace himself—."

D.L. interrupted. "I could take care of myself."

"—and disgrace the good name of the Holton Shoestore." Uncle Samuel puffed out his cheeks again and then sucked them in. "No, sir, Dwight. You're bright as a button, but you're headstrong. You stay right here in the valley and grow up to be a sensible farmer."

Then the sun went in. Everything in the world looked as sad and dirty as the brown hills beyond. In the distance, a train hooted twice and labored down the Connecticut River valley toward Boston. D.L. began to speak then stopped and, tossing back his thick black hair, he started for the house.

So his Uncle Samuel went back to Boston without him. D.L. stayed in the narrow little valley that every day seemed to get narrower. Some day it would

9

squeeze the breath out of him. It was not just the wood chopping. It was the farm, and it was the school. He felt as if he must burst right out of them to keep on breathing. One day, when the valley had smelled like spring for a week, he did. He packed an extra shirt and a change of underwear and, kissing his mother good-by, started for a town that he did not even consider second-best to Boston. But it was beyond the valley.

"Well, now, what is your considered opinion of our town of Clinton?" The old newspaper man who had hired him to address envelopes teased him every day with the same question.

"It ain't Boston," D.L. answered, not looking up from writing addresses.

The old newspaper man shrugged. "And you ain't Mr. Lowell or Mr. Cabot, either. Don't forget that, Mr. Moody, when you're feeling uppity."

One day there was a commotion in the outer offices. D.L. heard cross voices and then the old editor out-shouting everyone. He went on with his humdrum job. He was sick and tired of writing addresses but he consoled himself that Clinton was only temporary. Some day, he would be writing "Boston."

"Moody!" The old editor stamped up behind him. "That fellow that just come in, he tells me the papers have been going to the wrong houses."

D.L. looked at the editor, then at his list. "Huh?"

"Says it's the half numbers what's been complaining."

What in the world was the old man talking about? "Half numbers?" he repeated.

"Yeah, 51½ Walnut Street; 19½—."

"Oh, them. Why, I been figuring them in, all right."

The old editor stared. "Figuring them in?"

"Yeah. Adding them on."

"Adding!" The editor was shouting.

"Isn't 51½ the same as 52?" D.L. explained patiently.

"But 51½ is somebody's house. Somebody's paper."

D.L. was confused. "What kind of a house comes in half?"

"You never heard of tenements?" The editor didn't wait for an answer. "That's what I get. Hire a country bumpkin and that's what I get—51½ is 52! I should have known better. Country boys are hopeless. Moody, you're through!"

D.L. ran his fingers up and down the list of addresses, as if the smooth paper would reassure him. But the paper was flat and cold beneath his hand. "Half numbers," he said dumbly. "You'd fire me over a mess of fractions?"

"Once a farm boy, always a farm boy—51½ is 52. What in tunkit can I do with somebody that stupid?"

The road from Clinton ran two ways—back into the Connecticut River valley and ahead to Boston. For a long time that afternoon D.L. stood looking first one way and then the other. Then he turned and began to walk—away from Boston—back to the farm.

Chapter Two

WHETHER D.L. WAS CHOPPING PINE or picking beans, he could hear the hoots of the Boston train as it rushed down the green valley, away from

Northfield. Resting his ax or squatting silently in the middle of the beans, he would listen until he was not sure whether he still heard or only remembered its tantalizing sound. He tried to imagine what the train saw—the low hills, then the flat pastures and meadows and then the final wild rush into the city. And it was then—as he realized he could never picture the city he had not seen—that the hills seemed to move in until they almost buried the farm, the village below, and him too.

One day, in the spring of 1854, he threw down his ax. "I've had about all I can take," he told his brother George. "I'm leaving now." He walked down the lane toward the Northfield train station, but before he got there, he met his brother Ed coming up the hill. Ed argued, tried to coax, but D.L. listened with his ears alert only for the afternoon train moaning along the valley.

Suddenly, Ed quit. He reached into his pocket and then grabbed D.L.'s hand. "God bless you," he said. D.L. looked down. He was holding five dollars.

On the train D.L. sat up stiffly in the straight-backed seat and knew he was richer than he had ever been. He had five dollars in his pocket and he was on his way to Boston. The train rattled across the hills, and it was exactly like his dreams. The hills leveled into fields, and even the cows were fat and happy.

He yanked down the train window and thought he could smell the sea, even though it was still seventy-five miles away. The train poked through towns, and they were all bigger than Northfield. He was in a strange new world, and he touched the five dollars reassuringly. With all that money, he would not have to beg *anybody* for a job—just in case Uncle Samuel was not quite ready to hire a new man. D.L. pushed the uneasy thought from his mind and got ready to watch for Boston.

Court Street and the Holton Shoestore were a long walk from Boston's North Station. D.L. figured it was about as far as the pasture to the village church, but harder going because it was up and down hill and the cobblestones told him his shoe leather was too thin for city walking. But finally he saw it—his uncle's store, the sign swaying and groaning over the door.

His uncle was snapping the knot on a lady's parcel. D.L. walked up to the counter. "How's business?" he asked crisply.

His uncle stared. "What are you doing here?"

D.L. rested lightly against the wooden counter. "Happened to be in Boston. Thought I'd pay my uncle a sociable call first thing."

His uncle puffed out his cheeks, sucked them in. Then he spoke. "Now look here, Dwight, if you think—."

D.L. touched the five dollars in his pocket. "Thought I ought to pay my respects before I get too busy. Don't you want to inquire after your own sister's health? Well, Mamma's fine. So's George. And Ed. All of 'em. Ain't been sick all winter. They figure on having a good season on the farm." He stopped, grinning across the counter at his uncle.

"*They?* Dwight, if you're thinking of staying—."

D.L. felt the five dollars again. It was pretty clear that Uncle Samuel was not any happier to see him that if he had stowed away in his baggage last Thanksgiving. Well, with five dollars, a fellow did not need to beg for favors. Yet he did not move away from the counter, half-expecting his uncle to sigh, shrug, and then smile.

But his uncle was looking beyond him, toward the door. "Dwight, uh, customer. Step aside there, uh, now if you want to wait, if there's anything——," his uncle stuttered irritably. "Your Uncle Lemuel lives in the city, you know. I'm sure he'd be glad." Then his uncle smiled broadly. "Can I help you, madam?"

D.L. jumped away from the counter. "Don't mind me, Uncle Samuel. I'm going right along." He stepped aside for a lady in a green feathered bonnet, "Just wanted to bring greetings from the folks before I——that is——," he finished lamely.

But his uncle had disappeared behind the high counter, and D.L. heard his voice, muffled, saying, "Yes, madam, we most certainly do carry black leather in your size."

D.L.'s Uncle Lemuel was kinder. Apologetically, he explained he was not in a position to do any hiring, like Samuel. But he offered free lodging in his Boston home until D.L. found a job. Then he gave some advice. "First thing tomorrow morning, you stuff that pride in your pocket and go ask Samuel for a job. Ask him, point blank."

D.L. accepted the offering of free lodging, stubbornly refused to consider the advice and went up to bed.

The next morning he walked to Copley Square and thought it was the most beautiful place he had ever seen——the sun polishing the sides of Trinity Church until it shone like marble, the office buildings standing around in a cluster like farmers gossiping at the market. "Here was a city that would make a man big," he thought, as he looked through the square toward the center of the city and took his aim for the first office building. "People here know what they are about," he thought, pausing to watch a man help a woman from a high-step carriage.

So he began to look for a job.

"Experience, son?"

"Well, sir, there was a newspaper in Clinton."

"How long, son?"

"Well, sir, a week and then—."

"I'm sorry, son. We want an experienced man."

All the way around Copley Square, they asked the same questions. The second and third days, he started cautiously toward the middle of the city. But the voices remained just as cool.

"Education?"

"I went to school in Northfield and—."

"Graduation date?"

"Well, I didn't exactly—."

"I'm so sorry, son. This is an old Boston establishment. We are looking for gentlemen with educational attainments."

Nearly a week dragged by. No one had a job for him. Uncle Lemuel repeated his first advice. But D.L. was stubborn. He would not beg favors from Uncle Samuel. And Uncle Samuel knew he was in the city. But he felt desperate. A mountainous boil swelled on the back of his neck; he went from office to office with his coat collar turned up to hide it.

People in the offices smirked. "Where do you suppose they get them?"

"Off the prairie, looks like."

"That one must have walked all the way."

His five dollars had shrunk too. It was almost gone. But to Uncle Lemuel, he tried to swagger and say that he guessed he would be moving out to New York where he could have his pick of fine jobs. But Uncle Lemuel was not fooled.

"It takes money to get to New York, Dwight. Do you have money?"

"I can walk. I got enough for food."

Uncle Lemuel sank deep into an armchair and peered up at his nephew. "Walk? From Boston to New York? Sit down and let me talk to you, Dwight."

D.L. eased the coat collar away from his aching neck. He knew what his uncle was going to say.

"Dwight, sometimes a man needs modesty worse than he needs pride." D.L. shook his head vigorously, but the boil stabbed, and he hung his head limply, looking down at his hands. His uncle went on. "The kind of modesty that says he'd like to learn the shoe business if his uncle would be pleased to teach him."

"But he knows I'm here," D.L. protested. "Besides, suppose I ask and he says no."

"You have to take that chance."

"Suppose I don't want to," D.L. muttered.

"Then it's back to the farm, Dwight. That's the only way I see it."

Tensely, D.L. leaned forward. "There's always New York—." Then he broke off and sat silent, studying his hands. He was not going to callous them again with wood chopping. "Farm" bounced back at him from every gilt-framed picture in the room. He stood up and, crooking his head sideways to pamper the boil, he said, "I won't do it. I'd crawl all the way from Boston to New York before I'd go begging to Uncle Samuel."

There were two customers ahead of D.L. when he stepped up to the wooden counter in the Court Street shoestore. Only when Uncle Samuel had counted out the change for the second time did he seem to notice D.L. standing there.

"Uncle Samuel, I came to—I want to talk to you."

Uncle Samuel bowed to the women, handed over the change with a flourish that made him ridiculous.

Then, to D.L., he said gruffly, "Want to talk to me? Thought you would."

"It's—well—."

But Uncle Samuel was now looking happily toward the door. "You'll have to wait, Dwight. Customer coming in. Do you want to wait?" The sentence had a curious downward inflection, as if it expected a "no" answer.

"I'll wait, Uncle Samuel," D.L. said, his eyes on the wooden counter.

He moved away, backed into a dim corner and stood there, staring dully at a stack of leather pieces that smelled like the barns he had left behind in Northfield. What had happened to his big dreams? Nobody wanted him. There he was, his pride aching more than the boil on the back of his neck, waiting to humble himself. Suppose his uncle said "no."

But Uncle Samuel said "yes." Later, in the back room in the clutter of wrapping paper and string and old boxes, he grunted out something about family obligations and doing something for poor, brave Betsy. Then he grabbed D.L.'s lapels. As he talked on, he punctuated his words with jerks, and the collar of D.L.'s coat rubbed the boil raw.

"You're headstrong and cocky, Dwight. And wild as all get out. I don't like to see you coming into my establishment, and that's the truth. But you're my nephew and you're here so my course is cut out for me. But listen sharp, young man. You'll toe the line, or out you'll go.

"I'll choose your boarding house myself. You'll keep off the streets at night, and I'll make sure you do. You'll stay away from any amusement place I don't approve of. And you'll go to church every Sunday and Sunday school as well. You hear me?"

His uncle rushed on, talking, thumping, pulling

17

at the lapels for emphasis. D.L., swaying a little in obedient rhythm to his uncle's punctuation, did not protest. He did not want to go to church. Sunday school was worse. He had come to Boston to find out about cities and what goes on in them. But for awhile, he could put up with some minor frustrations.

The only things that mattered were these: he was in Boston, he had a job, and at last he was on his way to making something of himself. He might even make a fortune!

Chapter Three

"TAKE THEM OFF. The heel pinches."

From the back room, young D.L. Moody watched his Uncle Samuel amiably lose another sale. The woman crossly peeled the shoe from her foot, but his uncle smiled and said, "Yes, ma'am. Right away, ma'am. You know your own mind, ma'am."

D.L. turned to the clerk who was wrapping parcels at the long table. " 'Yes, ma'am. Right away, ma'am'! He couldn't sell shoes to barefoot Indians."

The clerk snipped the string. "He does all right, Moody. It's his store."

But D.L. was so sure it could be a bigger store, making a good deal more money for everybody working in it. Fast talking salesmen with push—that was all it needed. The woman groped for her umbrella; she would leave without spending a cent. D.L. sidestepped a pile of cured leather and caught up with her between the counter and the door.

"Beg your pardon, ma'am. I overheard what the proprietor said to you."

The woman hesitated. "Well?" she said.

"Now, ma'am, you liked those shoes, didn't you?" He did not give her time to answer. "You thought they were smart the way they laced up the front?" The words glided off his tongue. Behind the counter his uncle made nervous gestures with his hands, but the woman nodded.

"The way they tied on top?"

"Yes," the woman said and began backing toward the door.

"Now, ma'am, ain't it a pity to cheat yourself out of a lot of fun wearing pretty shoes just because your feet are too big?"

Uncle Samuel was stepping around the counter, but he stopped short. The umbrella twitched. "Young man, the *shoes* were too *small*."

D.L. looked amused. "All in your way of looking at it. Like I say, it seems a pity you have to say to your friends—no, I left the smart shoes with the little laces in the store, because my feet were too big."

"Mr. Holton!"

Uncle Samuel twittered across the room. "Madam, please—."

D.L. did not drop his casualness. "Sure, he'd be mighty glad to bring them out again. Try them on once more and see if they don't—."

Now Uncle Samuel had hold of his elbow. "I'm so sorry, madam. You see, the boy's new. Dwight, go to the stockroom."

What kind of way was that to take the punch out of a man's sales talk? "I was just about to—."

"The stockroom, Dwight. Madam, he's new and he doesn't—."

But the woman was gone, her umbrella stabbing an imaginary salesman in her path. The door slammed behind her.

19

What followed in the back room of the Holton Shoestore was not pleasant. Much of it puzzled D.L. He admitted he had not made this sale. The woman had even seemed cross. But he pointed out that he had made other sales, using the same breezy, unorthodox methods. He admitted he did not know one shoe leather from another yet. But he *was* selling shoes and he suggested his uncle look at the records if he had any doubts. He protested that he did not want to ruin the store. He wanted to get ahead as much as the next fellow, maybe more.

Cutting across the grass of Boston Common on his way home at six, D.L. thought over his uncle's scolding. The old man did not appreciate a young fellow's zip. And he had humored him so too, living in the boarding house his uncle chose, attending Mount Vernon Congregational Church down by the Charles River. He had stayed off the streets at night, like Uncle Samuel insisted. He went to Sunday school too. If his uncle wanted to check up on that, he could question his teacher, Ed Kimball. Maybe he was not the smartest nor the quietest fellow in the class, but he was always there on Sunday morning.

He was glad when he came to the other side of the Common. It always disappointed him that the city fathers had plopped this green pasture right down in the middle of what ought to be nothing but big buildings and cobblestone streets. When he was rich—the richest shoe merchant in Boston—he would change things. Smarten up the city a little. So D.L. continued home to his boarding house. He had been in Boston about two years. It was April, 1856.

On April 17 the sea wind blew fog and a few elderly gray-feathered gulls inland as far as the Common. The air smelled like burned coffee, as it always did on a damp Boston day. In Holton's

Court Street store, customers were few. D.L. slouched against the wooden counter, wondering if he ought to go out on the sidewalk to drum up a little trade. The method always seemed to startle people, but it worked.

Just then the other clerk jerked his head toward the store window. "There's a customer for you, Moody. Peeping in the window. Bet he's looking for you, Moody. Invite him in."

"Huh? Where?"

"The skinny fellow with the gray hair. There he is. Coming back again."

D.L. looked out and saw nothing but the watery fog. Then the gray-haired man paced by the window. It was Ed Kimball, from Mount Vernon Church. He would be a cinch for a fast sales talk. But what was wrong with him? He did not come in and he did not go on either. Instead, he paced past the store window a second time, then a third time. Swiftly, D.L. reviewed last Sunday. He could not remember any more trouble than usual in class.

But it might be better if he found something to do in the stockroom until Ed Kimball got whatever troubled him out of his system and went home.

He was yanking at the brown wrapping paper so energetically that he did not hear the footsteps behind him. But suddenly, he was not alone in the stockroom. When he felt the hand on his shoulder, he whipped around and came face to face with his Sunday school teacher.

"How d'you do, Ed? Uh, Mr. Kimball." He tried to tell himself that in the store he was a businessman in his own territory and he had every right to be treated as such. "Going to let me sell you a pair of walking boots, Ed?"

Kimball's face looked leaner than ever and gray

21

enough to match his hair. He did not smile. "No, Dwight. Not today, I—uh—want to sell you something."

It was good to feel like the master of the situation. Away from that stuffy little Sunday school cubbyhole, without his Bible, Ed Kimball did not act like the same man at all. Kind of nervous and twitchy, D.L. thought. He wondered if he were sick.

"Sell me what?" D.L. said, stalling.

"Not sell, exactly," Ed said, and his throat contracted. "I mean—uh—I want to *give* you something."

What ailed the man anyway?

"If you'll take it. Listen to me, Dwight. You don't mind if I put my hand on your shoulder, do you?"

It was not exactly how he would choose to sell a man a pair of shoes. Grabbing his shoulder that way gave Ed Kimball an advantage. D.L. shook his head.

The hand on his shoulder tensed. "Dwight, I've been trying to get up my courage to come in and see you. Dwight, I know you haven't thought much of my Sunday school class. I confess to God something. I haven't thought much of having you in it."

So that's what was coming? This was just a roundabout way to ask him to get out of the class.

"So, Dwight, I thought I'd come around here to ask you. Uh, that is, where I could talk to you away from the others."

"Ask me what, Ed?"

"Dwight, God loves you," Ed Kimball said abruptly. "His Son, Jesus Christ, died for you. Dwight, I want to know if you believe that. I have to know if you believe that before another Sunday goes by."

"Why, I—."

"And if you don't, I want to help you see it's true.

22

There's a verse in the Bible, Dwight. I got my Bible right here." The hand left D.L.'s shoulder and began to fumble in the left pocket.

It was funny, standing there with the wrapping paper, talking about sacred things, with the smell of new leather so strong. Half a minute before, he had been thinking about shoes and now, Ed Kimball was facing him with God. He had always thought Sunday school was the time and place to talk about such things. But somehow, he heard what Ed Kimball said to him by the wrapping table more clearly than he ever heard him in the Sunday school room.

So there was not any sense in being smart about it. He wanted to be honest. "Why, sure," he told Ed, "I believe what you said. Sure, I do. Nobody ever asked me point blank like that before, so I never thought much about it. But when you asked me—put it up to me—why, there isn't anything I can say but sure, I believe that Jesus died for my sins."

The man's face looked as if it were going to crumble and then he began to sweat around the corners of his mouth. But D.L. felt good inside, all light and bouncy. So he said it again, loud and firm. "Sure, I believe Jesus died on the cross for my sins. And you know something, Ed?" Now he put his hands on his teacher's shoulders and felt the rough wool of his coat under his fingers. "From now on, I'm going to try especially hard to live like I believe it. Like a Christian. You watch me and see."

That night, as usual, he cut across the Common. He was still thinking about the visit from Ed Kimball and he was not sorry he had spoken right out. He still had the light and bouncy feeling inside. Then at the soft brow of the Common, at the peak where he could see the Charles River beyond, D.L. heard a bird singing. Funny, he had never heard a bird on

23

the Common before. Or if he had, he had never paid any attention at all.

The next morning, his uncle called him into the back room. "Say, didn't I see Ed Kimball from church here yesterday?" he asked curiously. He shoved a carton of shoes toward D.L. "Here. Might as well be working while you're talking. Unpack those." His uncle straightened up. "There isn't any trouble, is there? I mean, you haven't got Ed down on you?"

D.L. said nothing, bending over to reach into the carton.

"Well, boy, what did he want? What did he say to you?"

"He had something on his mind," D.L. said, vaguely.

"Young man, if you're making a nuisance of yourself up there with those nice church folks—."

Then, half in, half out of the huge shoe carton, D.L. told his uncle about Ed Kimball's business. Embarrassedly he recounted what he had said to Ed.

His uncle beamed. "Well, Dwight, this is a big piece of news. This ought to make a difference around here."

D.L. laughed, uneasily. "I don't know about that."

"Well, boy, what are you going to do about this?"

The question puzzled D.L. "Do?"

"Do about your decision?"

"What am I supposed to do?"

Some of the pleasure began to drift away from his uncle's face. "Did you talk to Ed about joining Mount Vernon Church?"

"No," D.L. said.

"No!"

"I didn't know I ought to," D.L. told him. Join the church? He said he was going to live more like a

24

Christian. He had not connected church-joining with that.

But his uncle was demanding an answer just by the way he held the wrapping paper silent. "Well, I'll talk to the minister next time I run into him," D.L. said slowly. "Tell him to put me down as a member."

"Slow down, boy," his uncle clucked. "You chase into something faster'n greased lightning. You have to see the deacons."

"The deacons?" D.L. reached into the carton again for another pair of boots. "I'll see them Sunday. I always do."

But Uncle Samuel seemed determined to go on piling up complications. "You talk like a know-nothing country boy, Dwight Moody," he said sharply. "You'll see those deacons when they say so. They'll want to ask you questions. And they'll want some proper answers from you, not a lot of smart foolishness. You'll have to convince them you're fit to join the church."

His hands in the shoe carton, D.L. smiled to himself. Since he had worked at the store, he had discovered he never had much trouble talking people into his way of thinking. There was no reason to suppose that the deacons would be any different.

Chapter Four

THE DEACON ON THE END of the settee looked as ugly as old Widow Moore's bull and twice as short-tempered. The deacon standing by the fireplace reminded D.L. of a sick cornstalk, with his pinched-up, buttoned-up vest and his skinny little shoulders. Over by the door, a man flicked his watch chain up and down. D.L. wanted to say, "We know it's gold. You can put it away now."

These were the Mount Vernon deacons. D.L. decided they were nothing to fear.

Relaxed, he tilted his straight-backed chair. Two legs wobbled squeakily on the polished pine floor, the other two legs hung in mid-air. Hands in his pockets, D.L. thought that if somebody would light up a fire to get rid of the moldy smell in the walls, he could feel comfortable for the evening's business.

"Dwight Moody, you are applying to this board for church membership."

"Yes, sir," D.L. said. The chair legs squeaked an echo.

The man with the gold watch chain was asking the questions. "You come before us tonight for examination?"

"Yes, sir." Squeak, squeak.

The deacon on the settee pulled the flabby wrinkles of his face together and sighed. Squeak, squeak.

"Now then, Mr. Moody, will you answer——?" Squeak, squeak.

The deacon on the settee twisted like old Mrs. Moore's bull when he stepped on the nettles. "Mr. Moderator," the deacon whined, "may I suggest that Mr. Moody sit upright in his chair and place all four chair legs on the floor."

"Huh?" D.L. said.

"The noise is disturbing." Now the wrinkles were no longer flabby, but tight-knit and hard. "What a fussy old man!" D.L. thought as he banged down his chair legs with a final anguished squeal.

The gold watch chain swung back and forth like an overworked pendulum. "Mr. Moody, answer these questions briefly and honestly."

"Sure," D.L. said.

"You know you are a sinner?"

"Uh-huh."

"You have repented of your sins and you know that you now need forgiveness?"

"Uh-huh."

The moderator droned along. "And that forgiveness is to be obtained only through dependence on Jesus Christ?"

D.L. began to relax again. Nothing to be scared of here. The questions were all easy ones. Slowly he tilted his chair, caught the bull-faced deacon's eye, and settled down abruptly.

"You love the Scriptures and read them faithfully?" Of course.

"You pray?" Yes, he did.

Now the moderator turned to the others. "Gentlemen, it would seem that this boy is sound in faith, though limited in experience. But remember, he is only eighteen years old."

"Doctrine's important too." D.L. thought the deacon in the corner had been napping.

"We shall proceed to doctrine. Mr. Moody, what has Christ done for you, and for us all, that especially entitles Him to our love and obedience?"

The question that could not be answered by either yes or no caught D.L. off guard. Nobody had coached him or prepared him for it. He tried to pull back all the Sunday school lessons he had heard, but all he could see in his mind was Moses and the wilderness.

"Did you hear the question, Mr. Moody?"

He swallowed. Maybe frankness was the best way. "I heard. I don't know what to say exactly. I think He done a great deal for everybody, but I don't know of anything He done for me in particular."

Making as much noise as if he had sat in a whole

27

nest of nettles, the bull-faced deacon rose right up off the settee. The skinny-as-a-cornstalk deacon unbuttoned his vest nervously, shaking his head. The moderator looked at one, then the other. Everybody talked at once.

"Now, Mr. Moody," the moderator began, "did I understand you to say——?"

But the bull-faced deacon did not let him finish. "The boy's not ready. Told you so. Cancel the procedure. Waste of time."

Even when the moderator walked to the door with him, D.L. was not sure what he had done. He knew that he had been wrong, that somehow he had not measured up to Boston standards, and that he had not been given a chance to talk his way out of it. But he knew this: that his conversation with Ed Kimball in the shoestore had nothing at all to do with his interview with the deacons.

It was not until he was almost home that he wondered about the justice of it. And not until he closed the door of his room behind him did he wonder about what to tell his uncle.

Uncle Samuel, when he heard that Mount Vernon Church had declared D.L. unfit for membership, was angry. At first he stormed about the deacons, calling them rich Beacon Hill snobs, doubting their Christianity. Finally, he turned on D.L.

"You must have insulted them," he fretted. "Talked too loud or too long or rested your boots on the sofa in the church parlor. Or something that showed up your country ways. The doctrine business is just a lame excuse." Then his uncle eyed him sadly. "All the same, D.L., you won't let this make a difference in what you told Ed Kimball, will you?"

To D.L., it made very little difference at all. Joining the church was something he had his heart

28

set on—like topping his own sales record. He was sure he would get there eventually. He had been hurt some by the deacons but not enough to brood. Besides, he was too busy selling shoes. He knew he was a Christian, and he knew that the deacons too would know it eventually. In the meantime, he had his fortune to make, which did not seem to have much to do with either joining the church or what he had told Ed Kimball.

A busy summer went by. There was a new kind of imported leather in Boston, and folks had plenty of money to spend on fancy shoes. If D.L. bullied an occasional customer into spending more money than he had planned to, he managed to do it when his uncle was out negotiating for new stock. His sales record went up.

In October he applied for church membership again. This time, he knew what questions to answer and he kept his chair legs on the ground. When the session ended, the moderator crossed the room to him. "Well, young fellow, we're proud to tell you that you're ready and fit for membership in the Mount Vernon Church."

"Thank you," D.L. said modestly. "I'm glad to be a member."

"We think you're going to make a good one. Remember this, son: don't hang back because you're young."

D.L. grinned. "Don't worry about me, deacon. I'm never one to hang back."

Actually, he had felt at home for quite a while at Mount Vernon services. Since his encounter with Ed Kimball, he had attended even the middle-of-the-week prayer meeting, without being pushed to it by his uncle's conscience. When he became a member, he was there on the front seat every week. As a member in good standing, he knew he had a right to speak up at testimony time. He surprised even himself that he had so much to say.

"Folks, I been sitting back there thinking that the minute there was a lull I'd jump up and say what was on my mind. It seems to me that salvation is an awful lot like selling shoes." In the back of the room, he saw some quizzical expressions. "I see some of you looking like you think I'm crazy, but let me tell you what I mean. I sell an awful lot of shoes, so I ought to know. Sometimes a shoe pinches. That usually means that your feet are just plain too big. I fit some of the ladies sitting right here in this room and I ought to know."

He supposed that bad-tempered woman with the bumpy nose did not like that, but nobody knew he meant her. The more he thought about what he had said, the better he liked it. He went right on. "Like a foot's too big, pride can be too big too. And when pride gets too big, it means you have trouble putting on God's salvation." He took a breath. "Or maybe the shoe ain't fancy enough."

That was another dandy idea. He felt good standing up there, talking to the people. Some of them frowned up at him like they couldn't hear what he said. So he talked a little louder. "A lot of ladies sitting right here come in and say, 'Mr. Moody, I want a fancy shoe.' Well, I usually tell them shoe leather is shoe leather, and that's the way it is with God's salvation. It's plain and—."

Sometimes, his testimonies lasted for ten minutes, for fifteen. None of the whispers in the rows filtered up to him.

"How long has that impossible fellow gone on?"

"Somebody ought to do something about it."

"Before he ruins the church."

But the whispers did filter into his uncle's store. And Uncle Samuel did not have to listen very hard to hear them. One of his old customers stood in front of the counter one day and declared, "Now, I know, Sam, you have to expect so much of this from new converts. But your nephew is impossible."

Samuel Holton shot a quick look out toward the back room where D.L. was taking inventory. He lowered his voice. "Now, now. Dwight and I don't see eye to eye on a lot of things. But the boy means well."

The old customer did not try to be subtle. "I won't argue that. I'm talking about the appearance of things. Sam, we have Harvard men at our prayer meeting and bankers and some very nice people. And that boy rants and raves. He's very crude, Sam."

"Well, he sells shoes that way."

"He won't sell me any shoes that way," the old customer said. She turned away. "And shoes aren't religion. He has the two badly confused."

"What can I do?" his uncle said. "I can't send him packing. I've an obligation to my sister."

"You do what you think best, Sam." She started toward the door, flicked her eye over a pair of boots and marched on. "And do it quickly. For the good of Mount Vernon Congregational Church and—" her eyes went to the boots again—"and all concerned, Dwight Moody has to be silenced in public meeting. *Permanently!*"

Chapter Five

THE NEXT MORNING, D.L. whistled his way into the store, slamming the door behind him. He tramped firm and hard across the floor, hearing the clatter with satisfaction. He wanted to let everybody know he had arrived, ready to start a day's work. " 'S peach of a day, Uncle Samuel. Just now, up there at the corner of Tremont, something said to me, 'It's almost summertime!' "

"Dwight Moody, I have something better say to you. 'Shut your mouth and get some sense.' And before summer-time!"

"D.L. stopped halfway across the store. What ailed his uncle? Indigestion?

"Dwight, your big mouth will ruin my shoestore."

Something worse than indigestion was at the bottom of this. Cautiously, he edged toward the stockroom. But his uncle's voice trapped him.

"Yesterday, along about closing time, I had a visitor. A lady from Mount Vernon Church. A very respectable lady, Dwight. With jewelry and furs and a soft voice. She came to complain about you."

"I don't remember fitting any Mount Vernon lady," D.L. began.

His uncle stepped out from behind the counter. His voice rose. "Not about shoes. Listen to me, Dwight. She said you've made a nuisance of yourself in Mount Vernon prayer meeting. She said you've been making a young fool of yourself in Wednesday night prayer meetings."

What kind of a crazy story had somebody tattled about him? And why? Last Wednesday he had been as respectable as anybody else. He had even polished his shoes before he left the house. He clearly remembered last Wednesday. He had even testified that night.

"Listen to me, Dwight. Those are nice people up at Mount Vernon, cultured, and educated too. They don't want to sit and listen to some country fellow."

Did his uncle mean that folks did not want him to talk out in their prayer meeting? But he was a church member in good standing, the deacons had said so. Yet folks still wanted to keep him off—using his clothes for an excuse or the way he pronounced his *a*'s. He looked at a pair of heavy boots lying on the floor and he felt as if they were tramping across his heart. But he stuffed his hands in his pockets and faced his uncle.

"I've nothing to apologize about," he said stubbornly. "A prayer meeting's for talking. What else?"

"Not your kind of talking. And you're not going to do any more of it, do you hear? Ruin my store, will you? What possible kind of gratitude is that? I took you right off the farm. Now you'll ruin my trade."

"I ain't done nothing to ruin your store, Uncle Samuel," D.L. said heavily. "I did what Ed Kimball asked me to do. You and everybody else said you were glad. I'm a church member. It's as natural as swimming in water to say what comes into my head in prayer meeting. Everybody else does. If they don't like my style, that's too bad. I won't change it."

He trudged out to the back room to hang up his jacket. The sparkle had left the day, and his nose began to prickle from the acrid new leather.

But most of the day, customers kept him too busy for brooding. Yet he avoided waiting on any fine lady who might have lived on Beacon Hill.

On Wednesday night, the hymns had a beat and rhythm that kept D.L. tapping the floor and finally lifted him right out of his chair when it came time for testifying. "'Tain't nothing that we do that makes us look good to God. We all look bad to God unless we got Jesus Christ in our hearts. That's the way I look at it, which reminds me of something somebody said to me in the store the other day."

The next Wednesday and the one after that, somebody else just happened to remind D.L. of what had happened in the shoestore and must be told. So he jumped up and spoke out. Later, listening to the droning deacons, he knew what he said had more pep and ginger.

About a month later, Mount Vernon's minister, Dr. Edward Kirk, called him into his study. D.L. had never seen so many books in one room. Behind his desk Dr. Kirk dug a pen point into a stack of loose papers as he talked, pulling the pen out and then pushing it into the papers again. "Dwight, I'm going to be very direct. I'll not defend people or scold you unnecessarily. You know what I'm going to say?"

D.L. scowled. If Dr. Kirk's voice weren't so soothing, he would be sitting on the edge of his chair, ready to fight. Instead, he nodded.

"Mount Vernon is a society church. Many of our people live on Beacon Hill and have a good deal of money. Perhaps more than they should have. These people are—Bostonians, Dwight. You don't know what that means because you aren't a Bostonian."

"That don't make them right."

Dr. Kirk went right on. "These people like dignified organ music and stained-glass windows and proper English and restrained voices. They like their religion, their Christianity, to have these things."

34

D.L. slouched into his chair. "What do you want me to do?"

"I want you to respect these people, Dwight." The penpoint again punctured the papers.

D.L. bolted up. Dr. Kirk's soothing voice had misled him. He had thought the man understood. "Respect them!" D.L. exploded.

Dr. Kirk looked at him, kindly, as if he liked him. But he said, "Respect them enough to modify your prayer-meeting testimonies for them. Dwight, please understand. I'm asking you not to monopolize our testimony meeting on Wednesday. When you do talk, please don't shout." Dr. Kirk flung down the pen and leaned back in his chair. "And oh, Dwight, limit your anecdotes one to a testimony."

D.L. was on his feet. "You're asking me what my uncle asked."

"Perhaps. But that's the way it is."

"Bostonians got you running too, huh?" D.L. asked shortly.

Dr. Kirk shook his head. "No. I respect them. If the way they want to do things is part of them, then I'll—."

But D.L. interrupted. "Huh! They want to do things the way they've always done them. That's their trouble."

"Dwight, please."

"I tell you, Dr. Kirk, I'm about decided. I'm sick and tired of Bostonians and I don't know how much longer I can stand them."

He made no attempt to be polite to the minister. After he had bitten out the words, he went out of the study quickly. It was not until he was halfway home that he realized what he had said. At first he was surprised at himself, and then he realized that he had put into words what he had thought for a long time. He had tried hard to like Boston but, from the start, it seemed as if he had been out of step with the city.

He remembered a young calf at home, always frisking ahead of the rest or off somewhere to one side when they went to pasture and when they came for milking at night. That was the way he was too.

But a man could not sell shoes by sulking about his troubles in a corner. And D.L. liked to sell shoes. It gave him a great big powerful feeling to take the cash and watch the customer walk out, happy. To know that he had done it. To know that his words had done the persuading.

The shoestore was eighteen-year-old D.L.'s whole life. He even dreamed about it, waking up in the morning to grasp for what he had dreamed—ideas for a new shoe display, maybe. He always itched to try out new ideas. One morning, when Uncle Samuel was out, he arranged a display of shoe leather like nobody had ever before seen in the Court Street store. He swept the old chaste display of black boots into a heap. Deftly he arranged boots and shoes on a shelf together, contrasted for size and color.

Then he stood back to admire his work, nudging the other clerk for praise. "Like the way I changed things around?"

"Never recognize this side of the store," the clerk said. "Only wonder what your uncle's going to say."

"Huh!" D.L. shrugged. "Say now, that's sure an eye-catcher."

He backed to take a better look. Then he felt his uncle's hand grab his shoulder. "Dwight Moody, what have you done to my store?"

D.L. confidently, "Like it, Uncle Samuel?"

But the clerk muttered, "It was all Dwight's idea, Mr. Holton."

"You don't need to tell me that." His uncle's voice quivered.

"Now, Uncle Samuel. Stand back. Take a better look."

"I'll stand back all right—while you climb up on that ladder and take those shoes off that shelf."

"But—."

"Up on that ladder."

"But it's a real eye-catcher. Boots and shoes together so folks can see them all at once."

"You're a willful country boy, Dwight Moody. With a lot of crazy country ideas. In Boston folks don't scramble shoes and boots like that. It isn't done. Up that ladder now! Get!"

But D.L. did not start up the ladder at once. He gripped the rough sides until the little splinters pricked his palms. He was very angry. "It isn't done—in Boston—where a new idea isn't any good until it's a hundred years old."

"That'll be enough, young man."

But D.L.'s fury spilled over. He refused to dam it back. "Where everybody looks backward instead of ahead. Where everybody is as stiff as a frozen-over brook and twice as cold."

"Go to the stockroom, Dwight. You'll work there the rest of the week!"

" 'Don't talk above a whisper, Dwight,' " he mimicked. " 'There are nice people listening. Don't do anything different, Dwight. This is Boston.' "

"Go to the stockroom!"

He went. Halfway out, he flung back final angry words. "I tell you, Uncle Samuel, I'm sick and tired of Boston. Some day I'll find me a city where people like to laugh and don't mind talking ouᵗ loud. A city where I fit. A city where tomorrow's ideas are just as good as yesterday's cemetery. And when I go, I'll go so fast you won't see the dust."

That night, lying in bed in his boarding house, he heard the trains again, the way he used to hear them on the farm. The trains went west. They did not stop at the little Northfield station; they roared straight through. In his mind, he went with them across the country, to the edge of Lake Michigan, to the city of Chicago.

Every night he traveled west on a Chicago-bound train, for he knew something very clearly now. Boston—or at least what he knew of Boston—was too small for him, as the valley had been too small. It was too small for breathing.

Night after night, he lay there, hearing the trains, thinking. Then one day D.L. Moody went down to South Station and boarded a westbound train!

He did not stop in Northfield. He did not stop until he had crossed the Ohio pastures and the Indiana plains. When the train reached Chicago, D.L. was still on it. But Chicago was his stop. He got out, looked the city over, and found lodging.

Then in his new boarding house, looking down at the plank sidewalks across the street, and biting his fingernails, he wrote a letter to his mother:

September 25, 1856.

DEAR MOTHER: This is going to come as a big surprise to you. I have quit Boston. To tell you the truth, I was fairly drove out of it. I got sick and tired of all the rich and pious folks. And things at the store were not so good either. I came to Chicago and I think I will stay awhile. It is only a thousand miles from Northfield and that don't seem so far if you don't think about it much.

Of course, I don't have a job and don't know

where I will find one, but I will look tomorrow.

Your son,

DWIGHT

He knew at last he had found a place where he could grow big. The farm and the valley were behind him forever. It was all up to him now.

Chapter Six

MR. WISWALL, of Wiswall's Shoestore, flicked his fingernail against the big black leather boot on the counter. He seemed uneasy, as if he wished he were somewhere else. But his uneasiness and the paced tapping merely stimulated D.L. to talk faster and louder.

"You can't go wrong hiring me. I'm strong and willing. I'll tell you something else, Mr.Wiswall. I—."

Mr. Wiswall's nervous finger paused. "Mr. Moody, you've already taken an hour of my time. Monday is our busy day."

D.L. edged closer. "You know why you ought to hire me? Because I got ideas. Big ideas. Different ideas. The kind of ideas that sell more shoes."

To him, his voice sounded loud and confident, but Mr. Wiswall retreated a step. "I'm sorry. I have no opening for you. Maybe later?"

But the little man with the prim pursed-up lips and the full pinkish necktie could not dismiss him like that. This was Chicago. He had hand-picked this shoestore. And he needed a job.

"You can't afford to wait till later," he persisted. "Now look. I've been eying your display shelves, and it seems to me if you got rid of those boxes and

39

got your shoes out in plain sight, you'd be a lot better off. You need an eye-catcher."

Momentarily, Mr. Wiswall appeared caught. He turned back and picked the boot from the counter, rubbing his hand over the leather. "Shoes out in plain sight, eh?"

D.L. saw his chance. "I never saw such a dismal-looking shoestore. Why, if I had a chance, I'd change it around as fast as greased lightning!" He had tried out his ideas in Boston; he blurted this out almost before he realized what he was saying. When Mr Wiswall asked him a few direct questions about his success with them, D.L. had to hedge. Then he felt panicky. "I got to get this job, Mr. Wiswall." He ran his tongue over his full lips. "I got to make a hundred thousand dollars!"

"You—what?" At last, he had the little man's full attention.

"I came to Chicago to make my fortune," D.L. told him. "I set my mind to it. A hundred thousand dollars is what I want."

Mr. Wiswall stared at him a long time, pursing his lips into a tight little bow. Then he said quietly, "I don't think my store is the place for you. Not if you have your mind set on a hundred thousand dollars."

"I have to start somewhere," D.L. said, simply.

"With that attitude, you don't have to start in my store. I don't like the sound of your ideas. I wonder if you ever used them in Boston." Mr. Wiswall turned away.

Then D.L. remembered the letter. It had been in his jacket pocket since he said good-by to his Uncle Samuel in Boston. It might help. He handed the crumbled, yellowish envelope to Mr. Wiswall.

"Why, it's addressed to me. Who are you, young man?"

D.L. grinned. He should have tried his uncle's letter at the start. But it had seemed like taking a favor from his uncle. And he had wanted to get a job in Chicago on his own, for his own ideas.

Mr. Wiswall ripped open the envelope. He smiled, thinly. "Samuel Holton! From Boston! You know him?"

"My uncle," D.L. said.

Mr. Wiswall began to read. "Well, well," he said finally. "Now let me read this carefully. So you're old Sam Holton's nephew. Well, well." He read the second page. "Take off your jacket, boy."

"I got the job?"

Mr. Wiswall looked up, unhappily. "I don't like your looks, and I don't like your rough and ready ways, and I'm not sure at all you'll do in my store. But you're Samuel Holton's nephew. I'll give you a chance. Now come on out to the stockroom. You can start on that hundred thousand right away."

Now he was part of Chicago. He had a job and he had a start toward his goal. He was going to make a hundred thousand dollars. Quickly, he found out that selling shoes in Chicago was no different from selling them on Court Street in Boston. It was a matter of fast talk and nerve, and he had not lost either on the train ride west. In a very short time, he grew very fond of his new city. He could go his own way and be himself, and nobody cared.

Except Mr. Wiswall. He was full of advice, all meant to guide a young man along the straight and narrow.

"Keep your eye on the goal," he'd say. "It's the way you handle time off the job that'll make or break you. Got a girl? No? Well, you will have.

41

And you're bound to get in with the wrong crowd. They'll get you to spending money. You'll start drinking, staying out late. There goes your fortune!" Then he'd smile to himself, as if he thought that D.L.'s dream of a fortune was worse than ridiculous.

But Mr. Wiswall meant well, D.L. decided. At least, he never tried to put him in chains the way his Uncle Samuel had. He supposed it was just his curious way of encouraging a young fellow. And D.L. knew that, generally, he was right. He planned to take that advice. He would stick to his goal, he would make something of himself and get as rich as he could as fast as he could. But what he did with his spare time after hours was his own business, not Mr. Wiswall's. So were his friends.

He got in the habit of drifting downtown after work was over. Downtown Chicago was not like Boston. The street lamps stayed lit longer, and there were always people around. Sometimes he stood and watched the big carriages roll by, staring at the ladies with the fancy hats and the men who handled the high-stepping horses so cleverly

Folks were friendly in downtown Chicago. It was easy to strike up a conversation with almost anybody. And this seemed as good a way to make friends as any. After awhile, he began meeting a few of his new friends on a street corner almost every night. Pete and Mike, for instance.

"We wondered if you was going to show up tonight, Moody," Pete leaned against a store window, blowing smoke rings.

"Well, I was walking down this way so I thought I'd go by the corner and see if any of my pals were hanging around."

"So we're your pals!" Mike shrugged.

"Sure, you are." D.L. lowered his voice. "Listen, I got it all set for Sunday."

Pete rubbed out his smoke. "You never."

"Sure have."

"It's O.K.?" Mike asked. "Nobody asked no questions?"

"No questions," D.L. said. "And you don't pay a thing. It's my treat."

Pete whistled. "All I can say is you don't have much to spend your money on. Not if you're spending it on us, like that."

D.L. laughed. "That ain't your affair. See you Sunday."

Sunday was slow in coming. But finally it was Saturday night. As the clerks filed out, Mr. Wiswall stood at the door with his prim remarks. "Take care, boys. Jack, get some rest for that cold. Remember, Monday's another day. Moody, not so fast. I want to say a word to you."

"What's that, Mr. Wiswall?"

"Been meaning to say this for awhile. I like you better than I did, Moody. I'm not sorry I hired you. You're a good salesman. It wouldn't surprise me to find out you'd been saving a good bit of money since you've been here. But I can't be sure about you yet. You're not that kind. So here's a little advice——." D.L. kept his sigh to himself. "Watch out. Keep your eye on that goal. Keep away from anything else. Don't let anything at all get between you and that hundred thousand."

"No, sir."

"And remember, it's bad companions that'll fritter away your time quicker than any other thing. Well, Moody, have a good Sunday."

"Yes, sir."

43

He was a little late getting to the corner on Sunday morning, and he arrived out of breath, afraid that Pete and Mike had left, spoiling his plans for some fun. But they were waiting, and with them were some friends.

They all clattered along together down the plank sidewalk. Rough-housing a little, Pete pushed Mike off the planks into the oozy mud in the streets. Everybody laughed a lot and threatened to chuck Pete into Lake Michigan. D.L. felt warm and good inside. This was better than Boston. A fellow could never do this in Boston. But Mike was still nervous.

"Suppose some of your fancy friends sees us, Moody."

"Fancy friends? Who's that?"

"Your boss, for instance."

"Him! Forget it!"

There were five of them now, and the plank sidewalk rattled and groaned under them. Anybody coming the other way had to step aside to let them by. D.L. strode ahead. He knew exactly where he was taking his friends.

"You're sure it's O.K.?" Mike asked for the third time.

"Sure."

"And you're paying?"

"It's my party, I said. So don't worry."

"Well, I still don't know if I like the whole idea."

He stopped then in front of a squat brick building and pointed. They followed him up the steps and through the door. A man in a well-pressed suit and a soulful look approached them. "Gentlemen?" he asked, as if he resisted lending them the name. They all looked at D.L.

D.L. smoothed down his rumpled black hair and tried to swagger a little. "It's all right." He spoke directly to the sad-faced man. "I took care of things. My name's Moody."

From inside the building he could hear music, happy music. Everything smelled like good soap and flowers. The man was consulting a long list. Then he looked up and almost smiled. "Yes, sir. Follow me. All of you—uh—gentlemen—follow me."

"Come on, fellows," D.L. whispered.

The sad-faced man spoke again, "I believe you have the first five pews in the front. You are very fortunate, Mr. Moody. You and your—friends. I hope you appreciate how truly fortunate you are to secure five pews in the front section of Plymouth Congregational Church. It is really quite a privilege."

Chapter Seven

MAYBE IT WAS BECAUSE OF THE WIND, always blowing fresh ideas into the city and stale ones out. At any rate, Chicago was not Boston. And D.L. was glad of it. Could he have taken five hoodlums to the front pews of Mount Vernon church on Boston's Massachusetts Avenue? Not without giving the old deacons apoplexy and getting a Monday morning tirade from his uncle. But in Chicago, folks took new things in their stride.

It was even easier to sell shoes in Chicago. He never had trouble getting a good sales record in Boston, but in Chicago it was as easy as rolling off a log. A downstate Illinois farmer, for instance, did not mind talk about the size of his feet. What's more, he was not cagey and suspicious of a little high pressure, like the folks in Boston were apt to be.

Hooking customers from the sidewalk into the store did not raise any eyebrows in Chicago.

So D.L. pushed up his sales record, and his savings too. He could feel himself growing from day to day, getting to be a bigger person, moving along toward his goal. A hundred thousand dollars! He was smart, just like old man Wiswall told him to be. There was nothing in his life standing between him and making his fortune. His only recreation was going to church. And church-going never stopped a man from getting rich. This was hardly the kind of distraction Mr. Wiswall warned his clerks about.

For two years D.L. kept his eyes on his goal. He was so serious-minded about it that Wiswall's other clerks teased him. "Don't you have anything else in your mind but the shoe business, D.L.?"

"Sure, I do."

"I wonder!"

"I got a lot."

"Furnished room somewhere, maybe. You don't have a girl, do you?" they teased.

"I got a lot of girls!" D.L. paused, amused at their skeptical looks. "I spend every Sunday with them. All of them. But they're not the kind of girls you'd like. They belong to a Sunday school class."

"What!"

Then, perching on a big carton of shoes, he told them how he had spent most of his week ends for the last eight or ten months. It had all started when he was over on North Wells Street on business. North Wells was a messy street, with garbage stinking in its mud and tenements too tired to stand up straight. On one was a faded red sign that said: "Mission." One day D.L. walked in.

A man shuffled down a badly lighted hallway toward him.

46

"Saw your sign out there, sir. Thought I'd come in and see what it was all about. What have you got there? A kind of church?"

"Nope," the man said wearily. "Mission."

"Services on Sunday?"

"Nope. Sunday school."

Out on North Wells Street children clustered around every rotted front door. "You picked yourself a good spot, sir. No better place in the city to find children."

"S'what we figured."

There was a pause. D.L. set down his brief case. "Sir, I'm a believer in Sunday school classes. Fact is, a Sunday school teacher first introduced me to Jesus Christ. I'm a busy man—in the shoe business—but I got a little free time on Sunday. Tell you what! I believe in Sunday school classes so much that I'll come down here and teach one for you."

D.L. half-expected the man would take his hand and say gratefully, "My boy! God bless you!" But instead, he grunted. "Nope. Guess you won't. We don't need teachers. As things stand now, we got sixteen teachers—and only twelve kids."

With a dozen sweaty children fighting out in front of every tenement? "What's wrong with you?" D.L. asked bluntly. "You got plenty of kids right out on your front steps."

"You bring them in then," the man turned away.

D.L. picked up his case. "All right, I will."

The man turned back again. "Make a bargain with you," he said wearily. "You bring your own class and we'll let you teach." When D.L. did not answer, he went on. "And if you can't do that, you better not bother to come around here again."

D. L. went out and stood under the faded red sign and watched a little boy with a crooked arm

47

trying to throw a ball. Then he took his shoe case and left North Wells Street.

But on Sunday morning, he was back. The children were still there, playing the same games. They had not had a Saturday bath and they were not in Sunday school. The boy with the crooked arm was pitching the same tired gray ball. This time, D.L. leaped over and caught it.

"Hey, mister, give us the ball, mister!"

But D.L. held the ball, weighing it in his hand. "This old ball?" he asked.

The boy with the crooked arm came close. So did two or three others, looking mad. "What's wrong with it?"

D.L. held it tightly. "Ain't much good for a *Sunday* ball."

"A Sunday ball?"

Now there was a crowd around him. Little girls, bigger boys. With dirty necks, torn dresses, breakfast on their faces. "Seems to me, if I had this ball," D.L. said, watching them cannily, "I'd use it Monday through Saturday and hide it away on Sundays."

"Aw, we only got one ball. Give it back."

D.L. talked fast. "Then if I had only one ball, I guess I'd forget about ball on Sunday afternoon."

"Aw—." A couple of taller boys had joined the crowd. D.L. kept his eye on them. "If I was you," he said, I'd forget about ball and go some place special."

"Where?"

"I'd go some place where they were telling some exciting stories. Stories about lions in cages and men thrown in after them."

"Yeah?" The little boy with the crooked arm stood closer to him. "Where's that?"

"Want to find out?"

Most of them shouted, "Sure."

"Follow me. I'll take you some place where you can have the most fun you've ever had on a Sunday afternoon."

When he arrived at the mission, eighteen tattered children were still at his heels. At first the old superintendent did not remember him. When he did, he held the door wide open and tried to shoo in the children, saying to D.L. over their heads, "You kept your bargain. Come on in."

But D.L. stood on the steps. "I'm breaking my end of it. Getting a class is easier than selling shoes. Here, you take this class. Split them any way you want with your sixteen teachers. I'm going back for more. Go on, now. Get," he said to the crowd. "All of you."

"So, fellows," he finished, still perched on the shoe carton in Wiswall's back room, "that was almost a year ago. That's how I have spent my Sundays ever since."

Nobody laughed. Somebody said he supposed there must be a girl mixed up in it somewhere and he hoped she wasn't one of the North Wells Street ragamuffins. Everybody laughed, and D.L. laughed too and said she was not. There was a girl, and she was very pretty, but her father was one of the Revells who built ships out by the lake. Somebody whistled and said, "So that's it, after all."

D.L. grinned. "No, that ain't it. I ain't had much time to make much of a go with Miss Emma Revell. Maybe some day I'll get around to it. Truth is, fellows, I like kids. I believe in this Sunday school class business. It's the only way they'll ever hear that God loves them. Now maybe you'll leave me alone. I got something on my mind besides shoes, since you've been wondering. But let me tell you this:

49

selling shoes comes first with me and I'll skin anybody alive that tries to beat my sales record!"

He went right on making that record. It did not take long at all to convince old man Wiswall that he had been smart to hire Samuel Holton's nephew. When Wiswall added a jobbing department to his business, he promoted D.L. right into it. The figures on D.L.'s paycheck went up. So did his bank account.

And every time D.L. walked down the streets of Chicago, he knew he belonged. The city was growing, and so was he. If nothing got in his way, he might be the richest young man in the whole place!

For a year he was content with Wiswall's jobbing department. But one day he was startled to hear from C. N. Henderson, owner of another shoe firm. When he reached Henderson's private office, Henderson told him he was going to take him away from Wiswall. What he offered was a temptation.

" 'D.L. Moody, commercial traveler for C. N. Henderson!' How does that sound to you, D.L.?"

"Sounds good. But don't press me into saying yes right away. There are a lot of things a man has to consider."

"Come here. Over to the window, D.L." They stood there together, behind Henderson's desk, looking out from the sixth-floor office. Beyond was the lake, flat as a giant's hand reaching up from the city to grasp the wealth of the north country, a hand freckled by freighters and sidewheelers, some going north, some heading east. Henderson put his hand on D.L.'s shoulder and turned him around to look the other way, toward the south. Illinois land stretched out green and fertile as far as he could see. "It's your land, D.L. Down that way is Indiana. And over there where we can't see is Missouri and Iowa. Up there would be Wisconsin."

His land. The big new Midwest. His kind of land. He loved it already and he had seen only a fraction of it, no more than the city that was the center of it all. If he took the new job, all this could be his territory. D.L. Moody, commercial traveler!

"You'd see it all, boy," Henderson said. "You'd leave here one night and the next you'd sleep in St. Louis."

"St. Louis." It seemed unbelievable. A short time ago, he had thought he was trapped for life in the Connecticut River Valley.

"Dubuque, Minneapolis, Madison, Kansas City." Henderson named the cities as if D.L. could step out of the window in seven-league boots. There was no reason why he could not take the new job. Yet he had to be sure—about the salary, for example.

"Now what was that figure you quoted to me, Mr. Henderson? And about the expense account money. I don't quite understand that."

Henderson looked a little impatient. "The expense account is simple, boy. Say I send you to Minneapolis for a month. You keep track of what it costs to get there, and I reimburse you. But maybe you finish up in Minneapolis before the month is up. Then I send you off to Kansas City." D.L. nodded. "And once a month, boy, as a kind of extra bonus, I pay your way back to Chicago. From wherever you are, I pay your way back. Want to keep my eye on you."

At first it sounded good. Then he listened carefully to Henderson's word. What had he said— "once a month"? But he had to come back to Chicago more than once a month. He had obligations. He tried to explain to Henderson.

"I have to come back every week end. I have obligations."

Henderson was exasperated. "You're single, aren't you?"

"Yes, but—."

"Obligations? Boy, you don't have any obligations. Is there a girl?"

D.L. thought about Emma Revell. But he shook his head. "It's not a girl."

Henderson turned toward the window again. "D.L., I want you to sell my shoes. You're a slick salesman. But I can't pay you any more expense money than I named. Or any more salary. Now if you don't have brains to see you're a fool to put any obligation ahead of a step like this, then I can't do a thing about it."

He was surprised at himself. Nothing should interfere with a promotion, more money, getting ahead toward a goal. He had not planned that it should. In fact, he had planned exactly the other way. He had been so careful not to let anything side track him. And yet, to his own amazement, he was sitting here in Henderson's office, hesitating over a promotion. How had he come to this point?

He knew how it had begun, of course. It had started with the Sunday school classes in the mission on North Wells. Before long, he had become still more involved, almost without intending to. He had started his own class, so small at first that it met on a log over at the lake shore.

But it had grown. Now for almost a year, he had been holding classes every Sunday afternoon in North Market Hall. His friends had helped him. Sunday mornings they swept out the bottles from Saturday night's dance at the hall. Afternoons, they taught classes. More than three hundred kids drifted in from the slums.

He could not let these kids down. He had bribed them with candy to coax them to come. It took hard work and planning and large amount of salesmanship to keep them coming. And there was nobody else to take the responsibility for it. It was his obligation.

But Henderson did not understand. "I don't get it, D.L., I don't get it. What's in it for you?"

He hadn't thought about this. "I don't know," he hesitated.

"Why are you doing it?"

"Because I like kids," he said. "I feel good when I help them. This is the only church they'll ever go to. If I don't teach them about Jesus, nobody else will. I feel good about it, the way I feel when I make a big sale. Only better."

Henderson said nothing, staring out of the window. From where D.L. stood, he could see the sidewheelers humping along the lake front.

Finally Henderson spoke. "Then it's a toss-up. Do you like persuading a man to buy shoes and getting paid well for doing it? Or do you like persuading slum kids to read the Good Book—*for nothing?* That's your choice, D.L. Take it or leave it. But listen to me hard. Sentiment about poor kids or not, Henderson will give you one weekend back in Chicago every month. And not a dollar more. Well?"

"That's some choice," D.L. said simply. "I never guessed it would be so hard."

"Well? Yes or no?"

"I don't know, Mr. Henderson. That's the way it is. I don't know."

53

Chapter Eight

TIME TO THINK IT OVER, time to pray about it—that was what he needed. So he took the time, going to his Sunday school as usual on Sunday, talking it over with good friends. One of these friends was Colonel Hammond, paunchy superintendent of the Chicago, Burlington, and Quincy Railroad. With his whole weight settled on one of the shaky wooden chairs, the Colonel folded his hands over his fat stomach to regard the whole predicament with amusement.

"Well, well, D.L. Sounds to me like those two engines of yours are running smack into each other for a head-on collision. If you'll forgive an old railroad man for expressing himself."

D.L. smiled feebly. "Colonel, up to now I thought my Sunday school was a caboose. Nothing more than a nice little caboose."

Chuckling, Hammond rocked forward over his hands. "My boy, you got too much steam for the size of your engine. You start tooting down your track toward financial success and all the while you're stoking up the fires of this little old Sunday school of yours. And all with one hand. With just one hand."

Leaning against a stack of folded chairs, D.L. looked gravely down at the Colonel. Was he teasing him? This was a terrible problem. "I want that job with Henderson," he explained a second time. "But I can't let these kids down. A thousand of them—and who'll teach them about God if I don't? Colonel Hammond, am I crazy? I got my whole life to think about. I can't say no to a big chance." D.L. always shied away from asking anybody's advice, but now he needed it badly. The Colonel had created his own financial success; he was a Christian as well. "Colonel, tell me what I ought to do."

Colonel Hammond sat back and studied him. Then he spoke. "Take the job!"

For a second, D.L. could see a fat old engine, rumbling across a prairie grade-crossing. The Colonel was so sure, so blunt.

"My boy, a man's got one track in his life. If he gets off on a spur, he never comes back again. At least, not without losing five or ten years. You're on the right track. Commercial traveler for the Henderson Company. Take it, D.L., take it. There are big things ahead for this city, and you can be part of them, my boy."

Just then a little fellow with a runny nose and a torn shirt brushed against D.L. "See you next week, mister," he said. "I'm bringing my sister too. If'n my old man don't get hold of a bottle before lunch and keep us both to home."

D.L. looked hard at the Colonel. "You mean, quit the classes here? If I quit, they will too. My teachers mean well, but there isn't one of them—man or woman—with enough spunk and get-up-and-go to keep them coming."

"Not for a minute. Do *both*. Take the job. Keep your school."

"But I told you once. I won't have enough for room and board if I had to pay my own way back from—."

The Colonel was rocking back and forth again in some private joke. "Don't pay a penny. Hop a train and come ahead. That's all. Every weekend you get

55

yourself right back here to Chicago." He unfolded his hands and began groping under the layers of striped jacket and vest. "Here, got one right here in my vest pocket."

Mystified, D.L. watched the ritual. The Colonel was making elaborate preparations for a joke—or something. Finally, he reached the last layer, groped some more, and pulled out a slim piece of pink cardboard, handing it over to D.L.

"Boy, I'm not superintendent of the best little old railroad in the midwest for nothing." The Colonel said nothing for almost a minute, bending over his folded hands and rocking back and forth in silent glee. Then he spoke. "Boy, read that cardboard. It's a free pass. Yes, sir, when Colonel Hammond says you ride free on the Chicago, Burlington, and Quincy Railroad, you ride free and no questions asked."

It seemed improbable that the small pink cardboard was the answer to all the terrible questions. But it was. "I don't know what to say, sir."

"Don't say anything to me, boy. You do your talking to Henderson. See him first thing in the morning and take your new job."

Now he was surely on his way. Nothing could stop him, and he had the confidential feeling that he was also doing it all the right way because he was taking care of his just obligations to God. Something very deep had told him that he ought to get out there and tell those slum children that Jesus Christ had lived to make their sad lives easier and had died to make what came later a job instead of a torment. Now he could do that and make a fortune too. There was no longer any need to be ripped apart by that uneasy conflict, after all.

So, in 1858, the year he was twenty-one, he

traveled all over the Midwest, selling shoes for Henderson. He loved it. He saw Springfield, Peoria, Rock Island, Decatur, and Quincy. He had a line that sold shoes in all of them.

"Take Quincy, for instance," he'd say to a merchant. "She's a growing place—new houses and businesses and people coming in every day. Mister, you *can't* get overstocked. Won't be long before there'll be more people living in this here city than you got shoes. Mister, you better double your order!"

He talked the same way in St. Louis and Des Moines and Dubuque and Minneapolis. And he sold shoes. D.L. Moody knew how to sell shoes.

But on Saturday afternoon, no matter where he was, he stuck his free pass in his pocket and boarded a train for Chicago. And the Sunday school in the North Market Dance Hall kept on growing. It almost seemed to D.L. that he could sell religion like he sold shoes. Once in awhile as he thought about this he wondered if it were an irreverent thought.

And he enjoyed the weekends as much as he did the weeks. Why should he not? More than a thousand boys and girls were attending his school now. Some of the smartest men in Chicago were taking notice of it—men like John Farwell, wealthiest dry-goods merchant in the city. In fact, enough people were talking about it to make President Lincoln curious to see it for himself when he was in town. One Sunday the president stood up on the platform beside D.L. and said:

"I told Mr. Moody here I never saw anything like his Sunday school and I guess I never saw anything like him either. I told him I didn't want to make a Sunday school speech, but he got me up here anyway. Well, you're all in the right place and learning the right things. You practice what you

57

learn here and you'll grow up to be honorable men and women. And don't forget to thank Mr. Moody for what he's doing for you."

Up there beside President Lincoln, D.L. ran his fingers through his coarse black hair and felt proud. If his Uncle Samuel could see him now!

There was something else about the Sunday school and coming back to Chicago. That was Sunday school teacher, Emma Revell. At first, Emma's folks had been a little dubious about the fellow from the East who badly scrambled his grammar. Gradually they had accepted him. There was little they could do about it anyway, because Sunday after Sunday D.L. and Emma saw each other, at the classes, at the prayer meeting afterward.

At one of the prayer meetings, D.L. decided that it was past time for him to make his feelings known. Sitting in the back row with Emma, he whispered, "Ain't too soon to let all the teachers know about us."

Emma wiggled a little. "Oh, D.L.!"

"Why not tell them today!" D.L. blustered. "Teachers' prayer meeting is as good a place as any."

"How could you tell them, D.L.?"

He was half on his feet already. "Stand up and say so."

Emma reached out toward him. "Wait, D.L. Fix your collar—." But he was standing up, clearing his throat. "Folks, I got something to say."

The room hushed. His voice reached to every corner. "I want to let everybody know that none of the girls better count on me taking them home after this." He heard a few giggles and saw some frowns. But he went on. "From now on, I'll be taking just one lady home. The one sitting next to me, Miss Emma Revell."

He sat down abruptly and absent-mindedly started to flick mud from his big black boot, looking sideways at Emma, waiting for her smile of approval.

There were other satisfactions those days too. Between trips he was a regular customer at a local bank and, when his balance jumped over the five thousand mark, he felt as rich as John Farwell. He was on his way. Henderson had promised him that next year he would pick up five thousand dollars in commission alone. That was over and above his salary; triumphantly he planned to save every cent.

A month later, C. N. Henderson was dead.

D.L. came bleakly to the Revell's house and sat down in the parlor with Emma. "Will it make a difference?" Emma asked.

He rubbed his hands back and forth over the sofa's mohair. "Terrible difference. The business is going to be dissolved."

"But, D. L., lots of places sell shoes."

He looked up at her with anguish, realizing that she did not understand what he was feeling, knowing that she could not because she had not started with him in the valley and taken the train ride to Boston and been snubbed by Beacon Hill and then fallen in love with the new West.

"I was doing great with Henderson," he said numbly. "Traveling from Des Moines to St. Louis. I liked that. D. L. Moody, walking so sure right along into success. I was going to be the youngest man in Chicago to make my fortune. You know what I am instead?"

Emma sat there, watching him.

"A traveling shoe salesman without a job. Emma, it takes a lot to get me discouraged, but never in my life have I been so discouraged as I am now."

He was just another unemployed shoe salesman. But not for long! D.L. knew there was no use in sitting around feeling sorry for himself. Everything had not changed. He still had his big goal. He still had Emma. So he hustled around and found a good job with Buel, Hill and Granger, another Chicago shoe company.

That year, 1859, D.L. was twenty-two. He worked harder than ever. He saw a lot of Emma Revell. And in his spare time, he ran his mission Sunday school every week, pulling more than a thousand boys and girls out of the tenements.

Pretty soon he was sitting on top of the world again. He thought his life had good balance. And he knew where he was going. Eventually, he would outsell, outtalk his competitors. Some day, people would read the name *Moody* on top of a tall Chicago building or a factory or something.

He was so sure it would work out that way. Until the day one of his Sunday school teachers stopped into the Buel, Hill and Granger office to see him.

The man was coughing badly, so D.L. brought him out to the deserted back room, pushed a carton of shoes toward him and said, "Sit down there on that box, Mr. Hibbert. You look awful."

The cough scratched up from the man's lungs. "I'm all right," he tried to say.

"Uh-huh," D.L. told him. "I saw you Sunday. You looked terrible."

Hibbert bit back a cough. "What's the use, D.L., I'm—dying."

D.L. stared back at the man. He said nothing.

"It's my lungs. Had another hemorrhage. Doctor says I have to go east." He coughed again, leaning against a taller carton.

D.L. ventured, "If you're dying, you can thank God you're a Christian."

The cough dwindled away into a sigh. "God knows I'm a Christian. But when something like this hits—all I can think is—what have I done for Christ?"

"More than most." D.L. tried to keep his voice casual. "You've taught Sunday school."

"That's why I'm here," the man said breathlessly.

"You've been a good teacher."

"No. That class of girls—not one—not one, D.L. —." The coughing stopped him. D.L. waited. "Not one cares about Jesus. They're giddy young pagans."

"Now don't fret about that. When you're back east, you can pray for them."

"Not good enough." The man used his handkerchief. D.L. tried to keep his curious eyes away from the bright red spot. Then leaning weakly against the carton, Hibbert asked his favor.

He wanted to visit every one of the girls in his class and ask them personally to accept Jesus Christ as their Saviour, and he wanted to do it—had to do it—before he went east, for he was going east to die. He said he wanted to borrow D.L.'s nerve; he wanted him to make the visits with him.

D.L. heard this in dismay. "I've never done that kind of thing. I always figured it was for the elders. The ones that know more." He was a front man. He could get people into a church but when it came to probing into anybody's personal feelings about Jesus Christ, he froze. He had his limits. It was better to leave that kind of talk to those that had education or at least the wisdom that came with getting old.

But Hibbert, coughing, persisted. He needed a carriage, and D.L. could get one. In considerable relief, D.L. agreed to that. He'd be glad to drive

61

Hibbert to the girls' homes, anywhere in the city.

But this was not quite good enough. "You will see them with me?"

"But I'm no good—."

Hibbert's only answer was a desperate spasm of coughing. His mouth hung open, his eyes stared. "All right," D.L. agreed hastily. "I'll see the girls with you."

The trip around the city was as unpleasant as he had expected. He had gone into tenement homes before but he had concentrated on keeping things light, aiming at bribing the young ones with licorice, joking with a half-sober father, never preaching. But Hibbert had a sermon to preach in every home, and D.L. found himself sitting through them.

"Peggy, you need Christ. Without Him, you don't have life. Without Him, dying is—just dying." Hibbert had been talking for twenty minutes but the girl—Peggy—sat slouched in an easy chair with broken springs, flipping her hair back, watching Hibbert without any expression. D.L. thought it was time to go. Hibbert was coughing badly now and when he got his breath, he said, "You pray with her, D.L."

"Uh—." D.L. began. There was a pause. D.L. closed his eyes, tried to think about God instead of the tenement room. To his surprise, God was as close as He was when he talked to Him alone. So he began to pray, as if he were talking to a friend standing there in the room.

"Dear God, won't you explain to Peggy? Explain all the things we've been trying to tell her. Make her understand that Jesus Christ is Your Son and You let Him die just so her life could be different. That is, if she just agrees to taking Jesus Christ as her Saviour. Uh—Amen."

For a minute, there was no sound in the room but the man's muffled coughing. Then Peggy leaned forward. Her hands were quiet on her lap. "You know, you talk like you know God."

"I guess I do!" D.L. declared.

"You mean, because of Jesus Christ, like you said?"

"He's the only way we get to know Him." Peggy looked down at her worn shoe. "Do you suppose I could? Know God, I mean?"

D.L. looked at Hibbert. "Peggy," said Hibbert, stifling a cough, "God put it all down in His Bible. Let me show you right here——."

There were other tenements, smelling of sour beer and garbage. Sometimes a girl would keep them standing in the damp hall for half an hour while Hibbert explained why they were there. Sometimes a father threatened them. But they went on until they saw every girl in the class. When they were through, they knew that the impossible had happened. Almost all the giddy pagan girls had listened and understood, meeting Jesus Christ for the first time in the shabby tenements.

It was something a fellow wanted to remember, to wonder about slowly. But D.L. had no time. Hibbert's cough was getting worse. The doctor said he had to start east at once. The night before he left, the girls from his class came in to say good-by. And when they were all there, a kind of spontaneous prayer meeting began.

Peggy prayed. So did the others. Timid little prayers that said a great deal. "God, thanks for sending Mr. Hibbert to us. He told us about Jesus and we won't forget him ever. Amen."

Then they were all gone, and there was nothing left in the room but the echo of the prayers and the man's tearing cough. Never had D.L. felt so alone with God. For something that had been with D.L. a long time had also gone. It was gone, but he had no idea how or when. It was his prodding, nagging ambition. It was the ambition that had pushed him from the valley to Boston, from Boston to Chicago, from Wiswall's to Henderson's.

Now at last he had seen something better. He tried to put it into words. "Changing folks' lives— why, that's better than selling shoes. You—me too —we told those girls about Jesus Christ, and how He could get hold of their lives and change them completely."

Coughing, Hibbert said nothing.

"I never felt so good in my life. It was better than selling a gross of shoes and keeping the profits."

Hibbert started to laugh but his lips jerked in pain.

"I don't understand what happened to me tonight, Mr. Hibbert. But something has. When you get back east, pray for me. You pray that D.L. Moody won't lose sight of the blessing he got tonight!"

As he walked home that night, he knew that his whole life had been changed, all because of this week. He did not care any more about making a fortune. Suddenly he saw the whole business of piling up money for what it was—a trap. Fortune-seeking was a trap as narrow and confining as the Northfield Valley he had run out of. And now he was suddenly grown big and tall. He would forget about getting rich, setting a sales record; he might even forget about shoes.

There was only one thing to do. It was really what he had been doing right along, but with just one hand, as the Colonel said. Now he would do it with

64

both hands and all his heart and energy. He would be a missionary to the city of Chicago!

God would take care of him, if he trusted. Suddenly he felt bigger and taller than ever before. As he walked along the plank sidewalk, he felt far away, as if he were floating. In the glow from the street lamps, the mud in the streets looked almost golden. He walked head-on into the lake wind, feeling strong and powerful, letting the wind cleanse him right down to his heart.

Then he thought of Emma. What would she say when he told her that he was going to be a missionary to anybody at all who needed him, and he would trust God to feed and clothe him!

Chapter Nine

THE WINDOWS in the cramped back room of the Methodist church rattled as D.L. banged another nail into the wall. Just one more, six altogether, and he would have enough makeshift hangers for all the clothes he owned, or probably would own for a long time.

"I suppose, D.L., you're waiting for me to say it's very fortunate that the church will let you live here." Emma hopped about like a grasshopper, dusting, re-arranging chairs.

"Wasn't their doing," he answered offhandedly, aiming at the last nail. "YMCA rents this room for noon prayer meetings. Suppose they figure I'll do enough work for the meetings to earn my room."

But Emma had not finished. "But I'm not going to say anything of the kind."

She sounded cross. The nail poised, he turned to look at her.

"You can't live here, D.L. Nobody could."

And he had thought she had accepted his decision to give up the job and his boarding house. Obviously, there was more trouble ahead.

"Nothing wrong with this room," he said firmly.

She stopped dusting, stood there flapping the duster crossly. "There's no kitchen. You'll starve."

"Not as long as I got two good legs to trot me across the street to the restaurant." She was taking the joy out of it all. He was grateful to God for this practical solution to his board-and-room problems, a place to sleep in exchange for some missionary work for the YMCA.

"That place! You'll poison yourself."

D.L. turned back and studied the nail again. "It's cheap."

"You don't even have a closet." He said nothing. Hanging clothes on nails did not satisfy Emma. But she was not going to live there.

"Oh, D.L.!" She was going to cry, and there was nothing he could do about it. Except give up his whole plan, and he would not do that. Not even for Emma. He put the hammer down, crossed the room and put his arm around her. "I thought you understood," he said. "This is the biggest thing that ever happened to me. Now I'm free—to do exactly what I want to do."

"Free to ride all over town on that crazy horse of yours!"

But that wasn't fair. She was calling him crazy —like the papers did when they printed the picture of him on his pinto, recruiting boys and girls for his Sunday school. Emma had to understand. Patiently, he tried to explain again.

66

"Emma, don't you see? I got time now. Time is better than money. Time to get maybe *two* thousand kids to come to Sunday school. Time to go right into a lot of houses and sell folks on the idea that they got to have Jesus Christ in their lives. Time to go up and down the street and time to take those dull YMCA prayer meetings and drag people in and make something big of them. And that's what I'm going to do, Emma. And I'm so happy about it I could burst."

She said nothing, and he went back to hammer up the final nail. When he lifted the hammer, she spoke and her voice was very low but very crisp. "Just like you were starting a new territory for Henderson!"

"What?" D.L. said, not sure that he had heard her.

"*Get* two thousand. *Drag* people in. D.L. you don't understand. Finding the right way to tell a person about Christ isn't quite the same as sitting him down and putting shoes on his feet and telling him they fit."

Now she was off on another tangent. Just like a woman. This one made no sense. "They're both selling, ain't they?" he said, defending himself.

"This is religion, D.L., Christianity. It isn't selling shoes. You have to straighten out the two in your mind before your plan works." He watched her pick up her bonnet and put it on her head, a little crooked. There was no mirror in the back room.

"You going now?"

"Yes," she said softly, "before I say any more. Or see any more."

"See any more?"

"D.L., don't you think I know? You don't even

67

have a bed in here! You're going to sleep on those prayer meeting benches. D.L., this whole scheme just won't work."

"My back's strong," he protested. But she was gone, her bonnet bouncing crookedly as she hurried down the long church corridor away from the little back room.

His hammer limp in his hand, he watched her go. She was wrong, of course. This was no crazy scheme. It would work. He had the assurance of his bank account; seven thousand dollars would last quite awhile. Moving into the church had been a careful economical measure.

He had thought it through soberly before he had left his job. And where the careful conserving of what he had and his thrifty living had to leave off, there his faith in God began. If he used his time for God's work in Chicago, then God somehow would provide what he needed.

It was not a crazy scheme. It was a belief that had been growing and growing ever since the day Ed Kimball talked to him in his uncle's shoestore.

As for selling Christianity like he sold shoes—well, why not? That's what he was going to give to God— his ability to convince and persuade people. Emma was all mixed up. She was upset. After awhile, she'd see. He thought happily how good it was going to be to sell something as important as Christianity, bringing more into his Sunday school and putting a little life into the noon prayer meetings. For the time, these were his two chores as missionary-at-large to the city, and he could hardly wait to get started.

D.L. was so sure that a prayer meeting for businessmen right in the middle of a city like Chicago was important. So he set to work to make it so lively that twice as many men would come in every noon. He went to work in the only way he knew— standing at the door to "sell" his customers the minute they appeared.

"Help yourself to a hymnbook. There's the stack."

"Come on in and get yourself a place on the benches."

"The YMCA welcomes you and D.L. Moody welcomes you. Grab yourself a hymnbook and sit down."

He took over the singing with gusto. "Stand up quicker than greased lightning and don't look like your shoe pinches."

A short talk was his responsibility too. What he said was as direct as if he'd been telling a shoe merchant how to move his stock. "This prayer meeting can't grow if some of you old-timers don't change your ways. You can't play cards and gamble your wallets inside out and fool around with loaf-erish sports like that and expect anything at all to happen in this prayer meeting."

Probably he heard the murmuring from the beginning, although he pretended not to. A lot of men disliked the way he shoved the hymnbooks around and shouted out the tunes. More than a few objected to the sight of his clothes hanging on their nails and the odor of his lunch of cheese and crackers that lingered over the room. Many did not like having the ungrammatical, crude, young, twenty-four-year-old insult them. The murmuring spread and then diminished.

The unhappy ones stopped coming.

Distressed, incredulous, D.L. saw the project he was pouring his energies into disintegrate before his eyes. Attendance got smaller and smaller. Nobody talked about it, at least not to D.L. Then one day there was nobody there at all but one old woman.

She seemed to take a malicious, naïve satisfaction in what had happened. "I been watching it come to this. A few less every day, dropping off, dropping off. 'Tis a wicked city, young man. No telling where those men'd rather spend their noon hours."

Morosely, D.L. stood at the door, not wanting to look at the old granny on the bench. "I don't understand it," he muttered. "I spread the word around. I invited a lot of folks."

"Invited the wrong ones. Wicked men. If they don't want to come, invite somebody else."

He lifted his eyes and looked at her for the first time. Maybe this old self-righteous woman was right. He *could* invite somebody else.

"Where are you going, sonny?" The old woman trapped him with her voice. "What about prayer meeting? Where two or three are gathered together in the name of the Lord, sonny!"

He had been about to leave because of the idea she had given him.

"Give me one of your good talks, young man." The old lady cozily settled back on the bench. "The one where you tell folks how wicked it is to play cards and to like money too much. That's a nice talk."

That afternoon he was out on the street, walking into the stores and offices of some men he knew and some he did not know. All afternoon he passed along an invitation to the noon meeting. He knew how to judge human nature; he learned that when he was a salesman. Now he was out to judge a man according to age and dignity. He knew he did not have much of either. But if he hand-picked fellows about like himself—free and easy and relaxed— then he could fill up his prayer-meeting room again.

He followed this policy for days. And the prayer-meeting began to grow. Some of the old-timers came back, not very happily, and stayed out of loyalty and curiosity. But mostly the men who crowded into the back room of the Methodist church were the kind that did not mind sitting on the floor when there were not enough chairs and benches to go around.

The noon prayer meeting was a packed-out, full-house success. Everybody said so, and D.L. knew he had done his first job for God well.

Then it looked as if everything would fly apart. It was April, 1861, and a cannon ball fired in North Carolina tore across the United States and divided it in half. The states turned on each other, and D.L. in the North found himself thinking again about President Lincoln and the time they had stood side by side in North Market Hall.

"You *can't* enlist, D.L."

"Emma, you read what President Lincoln says. He wants men."

"You'd walk out on the prayer meeting and the Sunday school? After all you've said! The way you've worked!"

"The country's in an awful fix, Emma. Seems like I got to help."

"What about me?"

"People get married in wars. We could get married," he said miserably.

"You said that a year ago when you gave up your job. But we aren't married yet. D.L., are you going to enlist?"

He wanted an answer as badly as she did. He kept thinking about the president and then he thought about his Sunday school. Then he remembered the commandment: "Thou shalt not kill." He wasn't a Quaker, or was he? All he could tell Emma, standing there in the Revells' parlor, was, "I can't tell you right off like that. Nobody could. I have to ask God about it, and wait."

Eventually, he also asked some of the YMCA leaders about it. He wanted to do what was right. He wanted to help the president and his country. But he *had* promised God.

The YMCA came up with a strange solution. "Do both," they suggested. "We'll subsidize you."

In amazed relief, he heard them sketch their plan: they would appoint him as a kind of special chaplain to the northern soldiers. Since Camp Douglas would be located a few miles outside of Chicago, he could travel down there for a day, hold meetings, and be back again for his Sunday school and his noon services.

If the war lasted more than a month or so, perhaps he could hold some services right out there at the camp for the wounded. No, it would not be fighting, of course. But it would be helping the cause. Would he do it?

"I guess I will!" he told them.

While they were still pitching the tents and the first regiment was marching into Camp Douglas, D.L. arrived and held his first prayer meeting with the lonely, nervous men. Soon, the YMCA built a temporary chapel there, and D.L. found himself rushing back and forth between camp and his Chicago work.

It was tense, exciting, and he loved every minute of it. The days when he was afraid to speak to a teen-aged girl about Christ seemed a long time ago. Now, he spent most of his days either doing a kind of informal, unofficial preaching or talking to soldiers privately about what Jesus Christ could mean as a personal Friend and Saviour.

And the fighting went on. D.L. went to the front
—Richmond, Chattanooga, Murfreesboro. Officers
let him go right out onto the field where the wounded
men lay.

"I'm right here beside you, fellow," he would say,
kneeling down. "God's here too."

A moan. Then, "What's—that? A Bible?"

"Just like God is out here talking to you. Now
don't pay attention to the fellow lying over there.
Keep listening to me. 'For God so loved the world,
that he gave his only—.'"

Back to Chicago and Emma. Emma kept saying,
"When is this awful war going to end, D.L.? Maybe
it'll go on till we're old. I feel old already. And I'm
seventeen now."

Finally, D.L. answered her. "You're right. The
war'll go on, and we'll get old." He was already
twenty-five. "I don't see much sense waiting any
longer. Lots of people get married in wartime. Soldiers and other people too."

In August, 1862, D.L. and Emma were married
and rented a cottage on Chicago's north side. D.L.
thought there was no more beautiful war bride in
the North.

In October, he was off again to the camps. Then
back to Chicago to take care of Sunday school business and his prayer meetings. Then back to the front
again.

"Welcome to Cleveland, Tennessee, Mr. Moody."

"All I want is something hot to eat," he'd say.
"Then I'm all set to start preaching."

"These men need what you can give them. They're
just about face to face with some awful fighting."

"Show me the tent, and I'll show them salvation."
This was so much better, so much more exciting than
selling shoes!

In 1864, D.L. pushed the memories of a thousand dying men out of his mind when he took his new daughter in his arms. "Go ahead and cry," he told her. "It's a terrible war to be born into, little Emma. Everywhere men fighting and killing each other!"

Then in 1865, President Lincoln made a speech. ". . . with firmness to the right, as God gives us to see the right, let us strive to finish the work we are in; to bind up the nation's wounds; to care for him who shall have borne the battle . . . to do all which may achieve and cherish a just and lasting peace among ourselves and all nations!"

The war between the states was over. D.L. came back to Chicago to his northside cottage and, taking little Emma in his arms, told his wife that he was home for good.

Chapter Ten

EVEN BEFORE HE GOT TO the YMCA meeting, he knew about the argument. Stepping along briskly through the downtown crowds, he was bracing himself for the impact. Because he knew that the meeting to vote in new officers and make decisions about the YMCA building campaign was going to be a fight. And the fight was largely about him.

He smiled grimly to himself. For the last month, they had been drawing up the lines. Some wanted to vote him right in as president and hand him the big job of raising funds to put up a building to house the YMCA now bursting the seams of its rented meeting room. They used as their main argument the fact that D.L. had just built a handsome church for his congregation who had met so long in the North Market Hall.

But how the others had argued against that! He knew.

"That fellow pulled the dollars out of the tenement dwellers to build their church, yes. I suppose he rode his pinto into the courtyards and shouted up at the housewives. And they yanked up their kitchen windows and tossed down the pennies. How far would he get using those tactics to deal with our Chicago businessmen?"

He knew what else they said behind his back "All high pressure and shouting! And his English!" And then finally, "We'll fight tooth and nail to keep Crazy Moody from ruining the good name of the YMCA. He'd go off on some tangent all his own and make fools of us! Yes, sir, we'll fight tooth and nail to keep Crazy Moody from ruining the good name of the YMCA."

The part about going off on a tangent all his own—now that sounded exactly like Uncle Samuel back in Boston. It was a constant surprise to D.L. how many Uncle Samuels there were. And they were not all back in New England, either—unfortunately. These people did not seem to understand that a man could not do very much unless he did have his own ideas, use his hunches.

Well, whether or not he was voted in as president, he had already followed one hunch, and it had paid off. He smiled to himself with satisfaction when he remembered how he had walked into the City Hall on a hunch.

"But, sir, I didn't know that the YMCA had decided to build," the petty official in the tax-exemption office had said that day.

D.L. explained. "They haven't decided. But I think

75

they ought. Think they will too. Seemed like a good thing to have something in writing about not having to pay taxes on such a building. Might help their voting along, you know."

The clerk had asked a few more questions, covered several sheets of paper with notations and then fixed a gigantic seal to the bottom of it all. The paper and the seal meant that the YMCA's new building—when and where it was built—would be tax-exempt.

It had all been so simple, D.L. thought. But some folks were so surprised when he told them what he had done. Yet they were all pleased. And it all had come about because he went off on a tangent.

When he arrived at the YMCA, the fight was on. For almost an hour they had been wrangling over nominations from the floor. The small room was steamy from a throng of men sweating in irritation and frustration. D.L. stood in the back of the room, listening.

"Now election is a nasty thing anyway, and there are bound to be some hard things said." That was one of the old-timers at the noon prayer meetings, one of the men who had been replaced by the young fellows D.L. had brought in. "I don't dislike Mr. Moody. I just don't want to see him doing the job of fund-raising. If you vote him in as president, that's what it'll mean. He'll be your representative to big business here in the city."

"He got us the tax exemption, didn't he?" D.L. tried to see who had called out.

"Built the Illinois Street Church, didn't he?" He had two friends, at least.

But the man at the front had the audience with him. "Let me show you what I mean. Now the people in the Illinois Street Church are underprivileged, semi-illiterate, uncultured——."

D.L. did not want to hear any more. Some liked him, some did not. Eventually, they would vote him in as president or they would not. He would find out soon enough. It seemed like a colossal waste of time to lounge around in the stuffy room all afternoon when the lake wind was blowing air so fresh that it was bound to wake up a man's brains to do some constructive work. In a day like this he had always sold the most shoes.

He nodded to a friend across the room, told another he would be back after awhile and went out.

He headed for State Street, walking fast to let the lake wind blow the smell of sweat and the crackle of irritation out of his head. His first stop was at a State Street office.

"I don't want to sell you a thing, sir. I just want to tell you how to make more money."

The bloated man behind the desk moved back and studied D.L. coolly. "Young man, I know you. I've seen your picture in the papers. On your horse! How did you get by my assistant?"

But D.L. rolled right on. "I bet, sir, when you saw that picture, you never asked yourself how does a fellow as young as that get a chance to ride around on a horse all day, doing nothing but promoting his own Sunday schools. Stands to reason I knew something about making money somewhere in order to stop making it when I felt like it!"

"What are you selling?" The man's mouth was still drawn in a tight line across his face.

` "Nothing! Just have a way for you to make more money."

"If this is some crazy religious stunt——."

"This is good on-the-level stock."

"Stock! You?"

"Ever hear of the YMCA?"

"Of course, but—."

Then D.L. explained the financial plan that had been taking shape in his mind for weeks, had finally jelled on his irritated walk across town. Anybody buying stock would receive six per cent interest, at once. Later, the YMCA would buy back the stock, at more than double the original price. It was exactly the kind of opportunity D.L. would have liked himself in the days when he was after a fortune. So he was not at all surprised when the State Street businessman said:

"Glad you let me in on this, Moody. Now I have a friend and I'd like to let him on it too. I'll give you a letter. You'll need it to get in the door."

He sold the friend too. That afternoon he made a whirlwind tour, a record even for him. When he went back to the YMCA meeting, he was tired but very happy.

When he walked in, they were counting ballots. "Well, got back in the nick of time," D.L. said gleefully to his friend at the door.

But his friend was glum. "They struck your name off the president's ticket. They put John Farwell up ·or president."

D.L., remembering three hundred chairs his good friend John Farwell had once donated to the North Market Hall Sunday School, smiled. "Farwell's a good man. But I thought he was up for vice-president."

His friend shook his head. "They switched. *You're* up for vice-president. Farwell's teamed with you. But even that didn't satisfy everybody."

"What do you mean?"

"They put up another ticket to run against you. It'll be quite a race."

D.L. shrugged. Whatever the count on the ballot was, he had had a good afternoon. "Guess I'll go on in and say something," he whispered.

His friend looked distressed. "Wait—."

"Wait? When I got something to say?" He skirted the knot of ballot counters. It was not hard to get everybody's attention. They had been waiting for some excitement. It was easy to see they thought D.L. would provide it—win or lose.

"Folks, I couldn't hang around on one foot and then the other through all the haranguing. So I went outside to get myself a little air."

From the ballot table, a man scolded, "Let's make our speeches after the results are in."

"This ain't a speech," D.L. retorted. "It's a kind of report to fill in time. Besides, it's right to the point. This afternoon I went out and cast my net among some of the big businessmen." Everybody was waiting now, he could see, not knowing whether to laugh or to get ready for some preaching. He went on. "Well, it was pretty good fishing."

He paused dramatically, raised his voice and shouted, "Friends, I figure I got enough pledges this afternoon to build us half the building we want and maybe more!"

There was silence, then a buzz.

D.L. stood there for a second, reveling in their reaction. Then he held up his hand. "That ain't all. I got my eyes already on a very nice site of land. I asked some questions, and I got every suspicion it might be available."

Another buzz, and then the man at the ballot table straightened up. He began to speak over the buzzing, and gradually everybody quieted. "Men, here are the returns. The Chicago YMCA has a president. John Farwell. And vice-president—."

They knew before they heard. They began to clap and cheer. D.L. stood in front of them, feeling good, knowing they had been smart. They had the name —John Farwell—for president. And they had the vice-president who would go out and sell their stocks and raise their money faster than greased lightning!

For the next year, he did just that. His Sunday school—it was now a church as well, with its own building and its official organization, known as the Illinois Street Church—occupied some time. But he concentrated on fund-raising, convinced that God needed him to get the world's first YMCA building up as fast as he could. He barnstormed business offices, he sold stock, he asked for outright handouts.

Within a year the building was completed, and it was Chicago's handsomest. The auditorium seated more than three thousand people. There were small- er rooms for classes and prayer meetings. At the dedication, D.L. knew he had never been so proud in his life. They named it Farwell Hall—that was D.L.'s suggestion—and dedicated it to the glory of God and His Son.

Standing there, D.L. knew that this beat selling shoes all hollow. He had done it. D.L. Moody had done it for God!

But when the excitement of the campaign and dedication was over, D.L. was startled to discover that Emma was sick. At first, he blamed himself. "Here I been running around like crazy, Emma, and you half-sick."

But Emma would not hear of that. The doctor diagnosed her cough as asthma, and D.L.'s busy-ness had nothing to do with it.

Asthma sounded serious. Remorsefully, D.L. dis- cussed it with the family doctor. But after he left the office, he swung cheerfully toward home. He was going to be able to do something to make up the last year to Emma. For the doctor had suggested that the best cure might be sea air. Sea air meant an ocean trip, and an ocean trip could mean England.

And England meant that he could hear Charles Spurgeon preach. Perhaps he could even arrange a meeting with that elderly German, George Müller, who had done such astounding things by simply trusting God for all his financial support. When he got back to the house, he grabbed Emma and whirled her around gleefully! They would leave little Emma at home; it could be arranged with the Revells. God would supply the money; surely He would. They would go to England—because of Emma's asthma and D.L.'s dreams!

By spring, 1867, they were in Bristol, England, and he was bounding up the hills to the Bristol Children's Homes with the man who had built them.

"Ach, Dwight, you go much too fast. My sixty-year-old legs, they do not do so good in keeping up with you." George Müller puffed along at his side.

D.L. tried to slow down. In some ways, the old German was a strange one. Even a little eccentric. D.L. had expected to meet a brusque man as energetic as a new machine. Instead George Müller was turning out to be curiously peaceful, as if he had spent a good deal of his life waiting, developing patience, or listening for inner voices.

D.L. matched his steps to the older man's, and then they were on top of Bristol Downs. In front of them were three of the most massive brick buildings D.L had ever seen. They were so massive that they made the hill seem topheavy. These were the Children's Homes, built by just one man's faith. D.L. was impressed, and he said so, using the highest praise he knew. "Ain't no finer buildings in Chicago!"

George Müller bowed slightly, an old-world bow. *"Dänke schoen."*

Beyond the three buildings, D.L. saw workmen scurrying back and forth. Two more homes were going up. They walked closer to the foundation. The smell of the fresh bricks reminded him of last year when Farwell Hall was being built. Mr. Müller ought to know about that. So D.L. told him.

"Got ten thousand dollars from Cyrus McCormick just for the asking. He's one of Chicago's richest men, you know."

D.L. waited for Mr. Müller to commend him, but instead he seemed to be inspecting one of the bricks. D.L. wondered if the old man was deaf.

He went on. "This sure reminds me of my building project. I guess you and me have a lot in common. It's an awful busy time, isn't it. Sometimes I didn't stop from breakfast-time to suppertime. In and out of one office after another, asking men to give, and then—." He stopped when he realized that George Müller was not really listening. "That's why I wanted to meet you."

"How is that?" So he had been listening after all.

"How is fund-raising over here? I mean, I suppose you can give me a lot of pointers."

But George Müller said nothing. D.L. urged, "What's your secret, Mr. Müller? How'd you do it?"

Somewhere little girls were laughing at play. George Müller seemed to be listening to them or to something. Then he said, "I prayed, Dwight. I prayed."

"I know that but—."

"That's all. I prayed. No running to the offices to

82

ask men to give. Excuse me, but this is the truth. I did not ask anybody. Dwight, you ask for a hint. I give you one."

The old man stopped again, as if he were listening to the little girls at play. "This hint is not so much about how to build a building. It is more about Dwight Moody, himself."

D.L. waited, wondering.

"It is not so much what Dwight, one young man who is just thirty years old, can do for God. This is what I hear you talk about. How many businessmen you ask. How you run around. How you get pledges. It is more—*what God can do for Dwight Moody*. Do you see?"

D.L. shuffled his feet in the grass. Below he could see the ships in the port of Bristol, and for a moment everything seemed unreal and this old man a fanatic. Then he said quietly, "Sure, I see, Mr. Müller."

Eventually, he and Emma came to London because, after all, part of the dream was to hear the greatest of all preachers, Charles Spurgeon. But for a while, he was afraid he was going to be disappointed. When he found the church—the Metropolitan Tabernacle—he was almost turned away. No one had told him that he had to have a ticket to hear Charles Spurgeon.

But there were tickets left that night, and so he climbed all the wooden stairs up to the gallery and sat there, alone in the crowd, to hear the man he had admired so long.

Afterward, he was never sure what Spurgeon had preached about. But he knew he had preached to him—D.L. Moody from Chicago. He did not leave with the crowd. He sat there, praying, trying not to weep.

"It's a long way to that pulpit, God, but a preacher never seemed so close. And You with him, God. Telling me—what? Right now, it's more of a feeling than knowing. But You're talking to me, God. And I'm starting to find out why I came over to England. First, Mr. Müller, kind of strange, but still—. Then Spurgeon. I got to piece it all together, God. Show me."

After awhile, he climbed down the long wooden stairs again and went back to the hotel room where Emma was waiting. The feeling that God was about to tell him something lasted. And in this mood, he went later in the week to a prayer meeting at a private home.

There he was introduced to an intense minister with eyes that seemed to have burned great holes in his cheeks. The minister, whose name was Henry Varley, welcomed D.L. unceremoniously. "You're praying with us tonight, Moody?"

"Why, yes, I've been invited—."

"Then we shall meet God together tonight."

Someone explained that D.L. was in England to sample a wide variety of things—Spurgeon, for instance.

D.L. interrupted. "Don't call it sampling. I'm looking for something here in England. Something to take back with me."

Henry Varley did not smile. "Do you expect to find it at our prayer meeting, Moody?"

D.L said nothing, and they all went into the small parlor. Someone read some Scriptures. A man with a beard prayed. Then Henry Varley, with no introduction at all, began to speak. He spoke low, but he handled his words as if they were a goad for prodding people.

"We try hard. We fail. We are sure we can
84

succeed if we try harder tomorrow. We fail again. And if we succeed, it is only half success, half of what it would have been with God." D.L. listened closely. "We are all guilty. All. For I tell you to-night—*the world has yet to see what God can do with one man wholly committed to Him.*"

The prayer meeting lasted for another hour, but later, on the London street, D.L. could recall nothing more. All he could remember were Varley's words— "the world has yet to see what God can do with one man wholly committed to Him." Why should those words sear him so? Was not that what he had done in the back room of Uncle Samuel's shoestore when Ed Kimball had asked him if he believed that Jesus Christ died for him? No, he told himself as he deciphered a street sign in the London fog, that had not been it. It had been a beginning.

But when he gave up his job—would not Henry Varley admit that a man could not commit himself more wholly than by giving up his paycheck? Yet Emma's voice nagged him, "This is religion, D.L. This is Christianity. It isn't D.L. Moody selling shoes."

And then George Müller: "It's not so much what D.L. Moody can do for God. How you run around. How you get pledges. It's more what God can do—for—with Dwight Moody."

The fog was so thick now that he could hardly see where he was going. He could only hear his shoes scraping along the pavement, but this told him he was making some headway toward his lodging. Was not that the way it had been? Ever since he had left the valley, he had never been sure he was going anywhere unless he heard the noise, the noise that D.L. Moody was making.

Selling shoes or raising money for a house of God—in his heart, it had been the same. Back on the

85

farm, he had said he wanted to make something big of himself, and he knew he had hardly changed dreams at all when he began working for God, as he had called it.

Suddenly, and for the first time, he saw that it was not important how big he could make himself. Instead, it was what God could do with a very small Moody.

The world has yet to see what God can do with a man wholly committed to Him. The world would see!

He turned a corner, and to his amazement he saw the hotel sign bright and distinct. The fog had lifted!

Chapter Eleven

EMMA AND D.L. went back to Chicago in the fall. In some ways, nothing had changed. D.L. was still a self-styled free-lance religious worker, rushing from one job to another. He worked for the YMCA, he spoke at Sunday school conventions. He was responsible for the Illinois Street Church, organized from his North Market Hall Sunday School class. For the next two or three years, he was generally too busy to see much of his family—Emma, little Emma, and Will, born in 1869.

But D.L. had not forgotten Henry Varley, Charles Spurgeon, and George Müller. In England, he had exchanged old values for new; he did not intend to give them back. He had made a new commitment to God. But as he bundled into a friend's carriage one morning, he had little idea how much that commitment was going to shape his life or exactly what the world would see because D.L. Moody had made it. In fact, he was not thinking about such things at all. He was simply very cross at the owner of the carriage.

"Emma, this doesn't make sense at all. This ain't any joke to play on a busy man."

"Hush, D.L.," Emma murmured. "The driver—."

D.L. leaned forward, shouting up to the driver. "Where are you taking us?"

"Sit tight and you'll find out," the driver tossed back. "I got my orders to take you there, all I can say." The carriage bumped along over the pavement.

"It's just a joke, D.L.," Emma pulled at his arm.

"I don't mind a joke, Emma. But this smacks of maliciousness. I know whose carriage this is. He's one of the bunch that still calls me Crazy Moody behind my back, sure as—."

"Now, D.L., it'll take a lot of people a long time to forget what you were like three years ago. You've changed, and folks'll get to know it sooner or later. Besides, *you* always liked a joke."

The driver eased the horses over to the curbing. Before the carriage shuddered to a halt, D.L. swung open the door.

"State Street, D.L.? Now whom do we know?"

"That house, sir." The driver was pointing to a large, new stone-front house. "They told me to tell you to go right in."

D.L. helped Emma down the high step clumsily, his eye on the house. "They did, did they? Ain't no joke for a busy man—."

The front door swung back. "Huh," D.L. grunted. He had thought as much. The man he had expected to see was standing there.

87

"Good morning." Emma sounded much too sweet as they went up the steps.

The man in the doorway ignored D.L.'s gloomy face. "Come right in," he said pleasantly. "Watch out how you drip snow on your carpets."

Emma chimed in, fussing at him. "D.L., those boots—." Then she broke off. "The carpets?"

From the parlor, the kitchen, the pantry, came the shouts. "Surprise! Surprise!"

"This your birthday, Emma?" D.L. grunted. He knew it was not. "What's going on here?" He moved in to the room, looking around suspiciously.

A dozen men and women popped from other rooms. "You ought to know. It's your house," they all said at once.

More voices from the stairway. "Like it? Surprise!"

But this was one of those fancy new row houses on State Street. He lived on the other side of town. What was going on?

Then they told him. "Some of us got together and we decided you work so hard that you deserve a nice place to come home to. We decided you're trusting God so hard that maybe He's expecting us to do more than we've been doing. So we bought this house. For *you*. Here's the key!"

But he was nothing but a country boy from the farm. He did not belong in all this finery. He looked over at Emma. She belonged. He took the key.

"Carpets, chairs, sofa—and china in the cupboard, Mrs. Moody," somebody said. "How do you like it?"

But Emma did not answer. Instead she moved over to the mantelpiece and looked up at the painting hanging there. D.L. saw in astonishment that it was an oil painting of himself.

"Best artist in Chicago painted that," a voice in

back of him said. "I think it's a good likeness of your husband, Mrs. Moody. Even takes a few pounds off him!"

Emma did not take her eyes from the painting.

"Of course, it isn't exactly natural. He isn't moving." Everybody laughed, but Emma said, "I think it's beautiful."

"Well, D.L., what are you going to say? Don't tell me we got D.L. Moody short for words!"

He was close to it. "It's the most wonderful thing God ever did for me," he managed at last. "I don't deserve it. But God bless you all, anyhow. Come on. Let the ladies show Emma upstairs. I ain't seen the cellar yet."

They moved in almost the next day. It took him awhile to get used to the carpets and especially to his calm pink-cheeked image over the mantelpiece. But he knew that in some way this was all part of what God was doing with him. They were all very happy in the State Street house.

Yet his life had not changed much. He was away from home almost as much as he was there. Each time, Emma seemed more reluctant to let him go. She said that she was beginning to talk to the oil painting as if it were alive. He left the comforts of the new house reluctantly too, but he was always sure that God was sending him here and there to speak at the miscellaneous conventions for a purpose.

In this spirit, he went to the Sunday school convention at Indianapolis in 1870.

At Indianapolis, they scheduled him to speak at the early-morning prayer meeting. He supposed some folks who disliked his free-and-easy style of sermonizing had chosen the time. Folks would be too tired out to get up and hear him. The ones that got there probably would not care. He tried to be good natured about it but every morning he sat through dismal hymn singing and sleepy testimonies in irritation.

One morning, burying his head in his hands, he tried to endure with some kind of patience an especially tedious man with a nasal whine. Suddenly the testimony was shattered by a deep baritone voice singing lustily, "There is a fountain filled with blood—!"

People woke up. The man with the nasal testimony stopped, started twice, and then sat down. But the baritone finished the hymn.

"God bless him," D.L. thought. "Whoever he is! There's a fellow that doesn't hesitate to do things the direct way. Wish I could take him into all the long meetings I get mixed up in!" While he was preaching that morning the thought came to him, "Maybe I could."

After the meeting, D.L. brushed through the crowd. The old lady with a question about Ezekiel got a short answer. Finally, he caught up with the baritone. "You there, wait a minute."

The baritone turned. He was a pleasant-faced young man, about thirty. He looked as conventional and as easy-going as a small-town butcher.

"How do you do, Mr. Moody," he said. "I've heard a lot about you, and it was a great privilege to be here when you—."

"Never mind that," D.L. cut him off. "Who are you?"

"My name's Ira Sankey," the fellow began.

"Sankey, huh? Where do you live?"

"Newcastle, Pennsylvania. I just—."

"You got a family?" D.L. had to know.

"Yes. I have a wife. And there's also—."

"Any children?" D.L. interrupted.

Ira Sankey looked vaguely annoyed. "I was going to tell you. We have two lovely—."

"What's your job?"

"I work for the government. The Internal Revenue Department—."

D.L.'s mind was made up. He had one more question. "How much do you make?"

"Uh—fifteen hundred a year. But I don't see—."

D.L. put his hand on Ira Sankey's shoulder. "Sankey, you give up your job. Come to Chicago with me. You sing. I'll talk. Simple as that. Can't do as well as the government but I'll guarantee you twelve hundred a year."

But the fellow pulled back. "I can't decide just like that, Mr. Moody. I never met you before. I have a family. I have to provide for them. But—I will think it over."

A few months later, D.L. and Emma welcomed Ira and Fanny Sankey to Chicago and saw them settled in their new home. It was exactly as D.L. had said: he talked and Sankey sang. And D.L. talked more and more those days. Sundays he preached in the Illinois Street Church, and Sunday evenings at the huge auditorium at Farwell Hall. During the week, he went to Sunday school conventions or special YMCA meetings or wherever anybody asked him to speak. Sankey went with him, and D.L. counted on him to oil the wheels of every meeting with his voice. He thanked God for sending Sankey to him. Looking ahead, D.L. saw so many ways that God might use them together.

But he had not counted on October 8, 1871, some six months after Ira Sankey had joined him.

October 8 began like any other Sunday. D.L.

preached the morning sermon in the Illinois Street Church. In the afternoon, he tutored the Sunday school staff. He had a quick supper and did some last-minute praying about his evening sermon at Farwell Hall.

As usual, Sankey was song leader and soloist. But the evening congregation was restless. When fire engines churned by outside, people squirmed. D.L.'s sermon faltered and he finished it abruptly, without the invitation that was always part of his preaching now.

As people left the hall, more fire engines raced by. D.L. and Sankey got their coats and started to leave Farwell Hall. As they reached the door, alarm bells on the other side of the city tolled.

"First time in years I preached a full sermon without an invitation," D.L. fretted.

Sankey hurried along the aisle. "Don't worry about it, chief," he consoled. "Most of those people will be sitting in the same pews next Sunday night. You can reach them then."

D.L. said nothing.

"Go ahead, chief, I'll lock the door." As Sankey held the door open, the disharmony of the alarm bells blasted at them. And as they heard the throaty cacophony of the bells, they saw flames shooting up across the river.

D.L. stopped short. "That looks like half of Chicago," he said. Sankey locked the door behind them. "That's too close for comfort, chief," he said nervously. "We had better be getting home. Fanny'll worry."

They parted at the corner. D.L. said, his eyes on the flames, "Tell you this, Sankey, glad Chicago's so handy to Lake Michigan." Then he turned and started north toward home.

At midnight, he and Emma were awakened by a

desperate pounding on the front door. A hoarse-voiced neighbor was shouting incoherent things like "smoke" and "get out." Wide awake, D.L. saw from his window a blood-red city. The flames were miles away but a smell of death was coming in the window.

Somehow they got the children up and dressed and downstairs. D.L. figured that he could bring the carriage around, fill it up with furniture and start out. Little Emma began to cry; Will screamed.

Outside, frenzied frightened people rushed by, dragging furniture, carrying children. Somebody banged at the door. When D.L. pulled it open, a wide-eyed neighbor stood there. "Get out!" he shouted hysterically. "Get out while you can. The whole city's going. No time." Over his shoulder, D.L. could see a carriage at the curbing, loaded high.

Emma was at his side, tight-voiced. "D.L., let's go with him."

But D.L. held her back. "Don't panic," he spoke gruffly. "We want to save some things."

"No time!" the neighbor screamed.

"Take the children." Emma pushed them out the door. "We'll meet you later. Be sure they're safe." The crying children were loaded into the carriage. D.L. turned back to Emma. She was at the mantelpiece, standing on a chair, struggling with the big oil painting.

"Leave that be," he said. The flames were getting nearer. He had miscalculated. No time for the carriage or the furniture. If they got out now, they would have to walk. They could not save a thing.

But Emma tugged at the painting, sobbing, choking. "I won't leave this. D.L., help me."

Suddenly, he started to laugh. He threw back his head and laughed without control. Emma stared. "D.L.,—what?"

He said above the laughter, "'Ah, it's a terrible fire out tonight, Mr. Moody. And did you manage to save anything at all?' Why, I certainly did, madam. 'What's that you're carrying, Mr. Moody?' Only thing worth saving, madam. It's heavy but I don't mind. See, madam, I saved my own picture." He choked off the laughter. "Leave it, Emma."

"I won't."

"Emma, don't stand there."

With a great wrench, the painting tore from the wall. She was sobbing. "I can't lift it. I can't carry it. D.L., please!"

The smell of burning flesh was unmistakable now —a stench. "Emma, hurry."

She bent over the frame. The canvas ripped away. "I'll leave the frame. Take this. I'm ready."

"The wind—," he protested. "You can't manage it."

But Emma was starting out into the blood-red streets. "I'm ready, D.L. We'd better hurry."

He went first, head down in the wind, leading the way, not wanting to look back at their home or at Emma, carrying the fluttering canvas of himself.

They walked and walked, finding shelter eventually with some friends on the far north side. D.L. stayed long enough to make sure that Emma was all right. Then he started out again.

This was the city he loved. Out there in the middle of the awful night were the people of his church. Over on North Wells, the fire was eating up the shabby homes of the children he had taught in Sunday school. Somewhere out there were the people he had preached to that night. He could not sit down and wait for the end to come to his city.

When the morning came, he knew that he had lost everything. Illinois Street Church was nothing but a blackened skeleton. There was nothing left of Farwell Hall but some plumbing and some metal chairs. The home that had been given to him had been taken away.

He stood there in the dawn, knowing that today the lake wind would not freshen the city. For him, this was much worse than the day that Henderson died, worse than the Civil War. He tried to think about what God would want him to do, but he could not. There was nothing left for him *but* God. Yet standing there on what was left of the street, he found it very hard to pray.

Four days went by. At the end of the fourth, Sankey took a train back to Newcastle, Pennsylvania. With him went his whole family.

"Nothing left," he said brokenly at the station. "If we had only known—. Nothing left to Chicago but the ashes," he said and boarded the train.

But D.L. knew that Sankey was wrong. Turning away from the station, he walked aimlessly. The stale stench of all that had burned gagged him. He thought what he had lost—his books, his furniture, his clothes. He remembered the oil painting. Poor Emma—it was all she had left. And what was it? Just an oil painting of a fat young man, with thick pouty lips and rumpled hair.

But how foolish! Emma had *him*. He had Emma and the children. Why, he had saved much more than he had lost. Of course, he had. What he had given to God in England was infinitely more than God had taken from him in the fire. God had left him *everything*. And suddenly he knew that the Illinois Street Church would rise again out of the ashes. He knew too that Sankey would probably come back to sing again in Chicago.

Then he began to run—up one street, down another—as if he had an important appointment and might not get there on time.

Ten minutes later, he was standing behind the table at a downtown relief station, measuring men for second-hand trousers. Later in the day, he took his turn at the soup counter. The important thing now was to do what he could do for the others.

Chapter Twelve

C HIEF, I DON'T THINK they want us in England. That's the trouble."

D.L. watched Ira Sankey shred a newspaper over his study rug. "Meaning what?" he asked.

Sankey went on tearing the paper into small pieces. "Meaning that they got cold feet about your kind of preaching. It's too—," D.L. watched him grope for a word, "—too different."

"So the men that invited me changed their minds. That what you're telling me, Sankey?"

"Well, those three—Pennefather, Bainbridge, and Bewley—promised to forward our expense money. But they haven't. It's close to the time we plan to sail, and the money still isn't here. Why?"

For a few moments, D.L. sat behind his study desk and let Sankey systematically destroy the evening paper. His mind was drifting back over the three years since the fire. Life had gone on—as he knew it must the day he had put Sankey on the Newcastle train.

Within a year, a new church had risen from the northside ashes. He remembered his quick trip east to ask John Wanamaker for money. For the burned-out families existing in the miserable cellars of what had been their homes, the new one-story tarpaper-and-board Northside Tabernacle filled a desperate ministry. His worries about the fire taking away his work had been so foolish. In the years after the fire, there was so much to do that he had moved into the tarpaper church to live and sleep at the scene.

He had been right about Sankey too. Probably the baritone never thought he would sing in a tar-paper cathedral, but he had let D.L. convince him he must. Eventually, Sankey had come back to Chicago to move into the rickety meetinghouse, too.

D.L. smiled to himself. Sankey had been faithful. The next year, when the church and the city were almost back to normal, D.L. left affairs with him and went to England again. "And now he probably wishes I had never gone," D.L. mused. In England, he had preached some, gone to a good many Bible conferences to learn what he could, and accepted an invitation for both of them to return the next year for evangelistic meetings. Pennefather, Bainbridge, and Bewley had invited them.

Sankey was right about the facts. All year they had waited for expense money. As they planned the trip, the money had not come. Yet Sankey was *wrong*.

"Give me that paper," D.L. interrupted his own thoughts. "You ain't been so nervous since the night your melodeon busted in the middle of a hymn."

Sankey stuffed the paper into his back pocket.

"Now listen to me. I admit it's funny we haven't heard from Pennefather and the rest. I admit I was too fast to give away my bank account on the strength of getting the money from England." He

97

should have told Sankey about that before. But it had been none of his affair, actually. "Not a very big account," D.L. added. "Just four hundred and fifty dollars."

"Four hundred and fifty—! Chief, that's enough to pay for our passage. You gave it away!"

"Listen, Sankey. It's all right. We're going to England. That's why I brought up the bank account. I only lent the money. To be used while I was gone and didn't need it. Well, sir, I need it now. I'll ask for it back again. We'll use it for passage money. It's plenty for me and Emma and you and Fanny."

D.L. waited. Finally, Sankey looked up. "Chief, that's fine," he said without expression. "Fine and generous of you. But I don't think we ought to go without hearing from those three men. Four hundred and fifty dollars will get us over—."

"I guess it will!"

"But that's about all. Then what?"

Then D.L. lost his patience. "Sankey, we'll get to England. They'll take care of us. What else can they do?" He went on. "Go on, Sankey. Don't worry about my study. Save your breath for London. You'll be singing there yet."

They sailed from New York in the spring of 1873, and the trip over was rough. D.L. was seasick all the way. Emma had one of her headaches until they docked at Liverpool.

At Liverpool they went directly to the hotel. There was a letter waiting. D.L. opened it, grinning happily. This must be the answer to the cablegram he sent before he left New York.

He read the letter twice, giving himself time before he looked up and faced Sankey and the women, standing there in the lobby with their luggage. "Emma—Sankey—that cable—never mind—." He blurted out, "Pennefather died last fall."

Sankey's fleshy face quivered.

"Bainbridge died last winter."

Emma squeaked out something unintelligible.

Sankey managed, "Bewley—?"

D.L. looked at the letter again as if the words might change. "Bewley—died this spring."

Fanny Sankey sat down quietly on the nearest luggage. "What'll we do?"

"We can stop wondering when we'll get our expense money," Sankey said sourly.

"No time for talk like that," D.L. said shortly. He collected his thoughts. At least, they had their hotel reservations paid for. What did a man do in a strange country without friends? If he were a dishwasher, he washed dishes. If he were a preacher, he preached. Names whirled through D.L.'s mind. He had met so many people last year; if he could only snatch out the name of the right person to turn to now.

"Come on, you three. We'll go up to our room, settle down, and do some reconnoitering. That's what they called it in the Civil War camps." Nobody smiled, but they made feeble motions of collecting their luggage. D.L. marched ahead toward the stairs.

But in the room he felt squeamish, as if he might be seasick again. If only Emma would settle down. This was no time to putter with the suitcases. They might not stay more than one night.

"Put those socks in the bottom drawer, Fanny." Her voice fluttered across the room where he sat with the morose Sankey. "Everything's wrinkled. Look at this suit coat." Her voice rose. "Gracious, what's this? All wadded up in the pocket? D.L.

99

is this any good?" She came across the room with a letter in her hand.

"Don't throw it out. Put it to one side. Later, I'll—."

"Do you want it or don't you? Because if you don't—it's a letter, D.L., addressed to you. I don't think it's been opened."

He took it from her. Why did women cluck so at a time like this? He looked at the envelope, remembered the letter as one that had been handed him on the New York dock. He had discarded it as meaningless then. Absent-mindedly he ripped it open and began to read.

"Emma! Fanny! Sit down." He chuckled. "From George Bennett, eh. Good old George. Emma! Sankey! It's an open door for us in England."

They all stood there, wordlessly.

"Well, partly open, anyhow. It's from George Bennett, YMCA man, up in York. Listen. 'If you and your party [that's you, Sankey] come by York while you're in England, perhaps it can be arranged for you to preach.' "

Emma turned back to the suitcase. Sankey said, "Did you say—partly open?"

"Sure. Open wide enough for me to get my foot in." He stood up. "I'm going out to send a wire. I'll wire my old friend George Bennett. I'll say we'll arrive in York to start our evangelistic campaign immediately."

The wire left Liverpool less than an hour later.

Mr. George Bennett, secretary YMCA, York, England. Your letter received. I'm ready to begin.

(Signed) D.L. Moody.

By morning, he had his answer.

100

Mr. Dwight L. Moody, Liverpool, England. Religion at low ebb here. Will take a month to get ready.

(Signed) George Bennett.

D.L. read it and stuffed it into his pocket. Then he sent his final wire.

Mr. George Bennett, York, England. Will arrive with wife tonight. Sankey coming at end of week.

(Signed) D.L. Moody.

When he arrived in York, he discovered that George Bennett was as timid and discouraged as his wire. He was a small-town druggist who, in his spare time, was the organizer of a local YMCA that met in one dingy room over his drugstore. Bennett showed D.L. the room apologetically.

"I suppose it looks frightfully small to you, Mr. Moody. You being so used to preaching in your great Chicago cathedral."

D.L. remembered the great hall at the Farwell YMCA and the way the crowds had jammed it the night of the big fire. Then he remembered the tarpaper shack on the burned out north side and the back room in the Methodist church where he had lived on cheese and crackers. He said nothing.

"Like I told you, Mr. Moody, York's not the place for revival. Folks away on their holidays and all that. And besides——."

"Besides what?" D.L. thought that Bennett was growing increasingly uneasy.

"If you'll pardon me for saying so, sir, I know you're frightfully popular over in America, but the Englishmen, well, they're a queer bunch. They like things calm and easy and with a good bit of dignity. Us nonconformists don't stand much of a show. I—well, sir—I just don't know how York is going to take to your preaching or how many will come to hear you. If you'll pardon me for saying so, sir."

The world has yet to see what God can do with one man wholly committed to Him. He had heard *that* in England, had he not? D.L. started down the stairs from the dingy room.

George Bennett was right. York was no place for a nonconformist. When D.L. jumped up to start off his first meeting, only eight men sat in embarrassment in the upstairs room.

But Sankey pumped away at the melodeon as if three thousand were listening to his music. When he sang, all eight men closed their eyes and seemed to pray. Then D.L. preached in his blunt way, prancing a little in spite of the confinement of the room, shouting too loudly for the little space, but weaving the Gospel truth into his homely stories as he always did.

The next night about a dozen men climbed the stairs to the room over the drugstore. "It's the holidays, Mr. Moody. I'm almost certain it's the holidays," George Bennett apologized.

But each night, a few more squeezed into the small room. It seemed to D.L. as if they were accepting him for what he was. After awhile, one nonconformist minister opened up his small chapel to the preaching and singing and D.L. felt happier. He pranced higher and wider, and Sankey pumped so hard at the melodeon that people in the square heard the music.

Five weeks went by—five weeks of preaching, volunteeer collections that paid for food and lodging, and five weeks of men and women finding Jesus Christ as Saviour. Actually, more than two hundred and fifty were converted in the town of York.

But something was not right. D.L. knew it. Sankey knew it. George Bennett had been afraid of it from the start. The people who did not come to the meetings, and some that did, spread stories. They mimicked D.L.'s shouting. They imitated the ruddy-faced man at the wheeze box. More damaging than that, they exaggerated the drama of a conversion to Christ until the meetings were pictured as a hodge-podge of hysterics. And while the ordinary man on the street loitered curiously outside their lodgings to hear Sankey practice, the ministers of York never officially recognized that D.L. was preaching there.

Bad reports spread about the countryside, into the small towns in which D.L. had hoped to preach next. In Sunderland, where he had been invited by a minister named Rees, trouble rumbled before he arrived. D.L. was not unaware of what was happening.

In Sunderland Rees had considerable difficulty with the spokesman for the local clergy. At first, Rees argued that in York the YMCA had sponsored D.L. But the spokesman would have none of that.

"Hah! The YMCA! A handful of down-at-the-heel nonconformists. Rees, I've got nothing but bad reports of what went on over there. Sensationalisms in all the meetings. All that fast-tempoed singing. That American tax collector waving his arms about like a madman. The excess of emotions."

Rees was firm. "All badly overdrawn."

"He lacerates the mother tongue. 'He don't.' 'Ain't.' From behind the sacred desk."

"But he has got a message. He preaches a pure Gospel," Rees insisted.

"Perhaps. But he parades under false colors. This buffoon from the far west of North America is not a clergyman. Holy hands have never been laid on him. The only consecration to the holy office he attempts to pre-empt is one that he made himself. He comes unendorsed by anybody of good repute, totally unheralded except by those dreadful reports from York."

The clergyman laced his fingers together and munched his lower lip. "Wire him not to come."

"My church is open to him. I want Moody in Sunderland."

The clergyman stood up. "All right. I have no intention of co-operating. Nor do the others. I shall not announce his presence from my pulpit."

D.L. and Sankey went to Sunderland. From the start, D.L. felt more uneasy about Mr. Rees than he felt about his own preaching. Mr. Rees was so worried about what people were thinking. He was so upset when a good many did not care for the two Americans. He went pale when he heard what they said about Moody and Sankey.

"Toss out the Gospel into the crowds as if they were hoping somebody might happen to get hit with it."

"Solo singing is not worship. It's a parade of human conceit. It's distracting, irreverent."

But Sankey's baritone filled the little chapel. D.L. told the Gospel the only way he knew how—with no frills. If they would hear him out, get used to the way he pronounced his *a*'s, he maintained, they'd like what he was saying and come back for more. He stayed in Sunderland and kept on preaching.

He did not stop even when the ministers of the city covered the public buildings with printed material, warning everybody about the Americans. "Kindly reflections on the present religious movement," the pamphlets said. "Part one, questionable procedure. Part two, probable evil results."

104

"Chief," Sankey asked him, "this represents some of the most responsible people in Sunderland. Do you think we ought to—?"

D.L. interrupted. "We know we're doing right. These men are two centuries behind Boston. Pity them and keep on singing, Sankey."

There had been so many in his life who had questioned his different ways—Uncle Samuel, at first, the YMCA men in Chicago, so many others. Eventually they all had to admit that he got things done in his own way and got them done successfully too. He would just ride out this tide also.

But one morning, Emma handed him another pamphlet. " 'Religious dissipation: a word of caution for this time of revival,' " he read. "Won't they ever stop?" he said and put the pamphlet down. But Emma wanted him to read on.

"Written by—why, it's Mr. Rees, Emma!" Stunned he read Rees' text: " 'Hast thou found honey, eat as much as is sufficient for thee lest thou be filled therewith and vomit it.' "

"He wrote that about you, D.L." Emma's voice was small.

"Then Rees—why, he doesn't understand me any more than the rest!"

"They're all against you now, D.L."

"Emma, why did this happen? Why?" The man who had invited him had turned against him. Why? "Ain't the crowds coming?" he asked her in anguish. "Ain't people getting saved?"

"Yes, D.L., yes." She came across the room and tried to put her arm around him but he pulled away.

"How can it be?" This was so unfair. "I turned myself over to God and told Him to use me. Didn't I, Emma? Didn't I?"

But she was crying now, her face in her arms.

He took the pamphlet in his fingers, folded it until it was a small ball and then threw it on the floor. He could give up now, go home, retreat in bitterness, asking the question of God, "Didn't I tell You to use me?"

But that first question had already gone. Another had taken its place. "Emma," he asked, "how long are folks going to hear my bad grammar instead of seeing Christ when I preach? When are they going to wake up?"

As he looked at her uplifted face, he realized all the hope that his question had implied. And he knew that even this awful thing had not shaken him from the commitment he had made that night in England, five long years ago.

Chapter Thirteen

WHAT HAPPENED IN SUNDERLAND was not a success by anybody's definition. But D.L. was not going back to the United States yet. When he was invited to preach in Newcastle next, he accepted. There, things were slightly better. At least, the opposition was not organized. At the meetings, many people confronted Jesus Christ in the inquiry rooms.

At Newcastle, D.L. was invited to go on to Scotland. A man named Dr. Horatius Bonar invited him to preach in Edinburgh. D.L. was elated. So was Sankey. As they packed the melodeon, they had no idea that trouble was already ahead of them.

In Edinburgh, Dr. Bonar was having his problems with a kindly old deacon whose Scottish tongue stuttered in anger. "It's not Moody I object to as much as the big-voiced one he brings with him. What that one does is an abomination in the tabernacle of the Most High!"

"I grant Sankey sings a different kind of music," Dr. Bonar said, soothingly.

"In the first place, he sings hardly any psalms at all. The ones he does sing are incorrect translations. I won't call it music at all. What he brings to the sanctuary suggests performances in places less religious than churches and chapels, dear Dr. Bonar."

Horatius Bonar was concerned. The good deacon echoed what half the church people in Edinburgh were saying. It was too bad that young Moody had no formal theological training to his credit, for Scottish churches were very strict about their clerics' credentials. But the music was the real stumbling block.

The deacon stuttered on. "Worst of all, it's what he brings with him right into the kirk. That—that devilish kist fu' o' whustles."

Dr. Bonar was thinking quickly. "You object to Sankey's melodeon?"

"It's an instrument, Dr. Bonar. An instrument in the house of the Lord. You're a Scotsman and you were reared to frown on such goings on."

"But these are Americans, deacon. Their ways aren't ours."

"A kist fu' o' whustles. A devilish pump machine that wheezes out blasphemously."

Nimbly, Horatius Bonar pounced on the only possible argument. He put his hand reassuringly on the deacon's arm. "You're right," he said softly. "I am a Scotsman and I have been reared to hold that

107

some things are wrong. But I have *seen* Sankey's melodeon."

The deacon's arm twitched but he did not move away. "What difference does that make?"

"Because this instrument is a very small one. It can't be a very *big* abomination in the house of the Lord because it is a very *small* instrument."

The argument considerably calmed the worried deacon. So Horatius Bonar used the same tactics on the other tradition-bound Scotsmen who came to say that they felt that they only sinned a little by agreeing to a *very small* instrument in their sanctuaries.

In November, 1873, D.L. and Sankey arrived in Edinburgh. From the start disaster dogged them. Six hours after they arrived, D.L. stretched out in the easy chair in the hotel room, eyes watering, nose running, voice hoarse. He shuddered through a spasm of sneezes. "I can't preach tonight, Sankey," he said.

Sankey sat down on the edge of the bed. "Chief, you never said that before. You have to preach. It's our first meeting."

There was another paroxysm of sneezes. "No use, Sankey," D.L. gasped. He always bragged that he was as healthy as an ox. But tonight he could not talk; he could hardly breathe. "You'll have to go out and hunt up a substitute."

Later that night, as D.L. sneezed disconsolately into a soaking handkerchief, Sankey told him that the audience had sat passively when he announced the substitution. A few had walked out.

But the next morning, the cold was gone. In the carriage from hotel to church, D.L. was exultant. "Must have been a bug that blew in off the moor.

Feel like a new man today. Fever gone. Congestion cleared up."

"Praise the Lord, chief. I wouldn't want another night like last night."

"We'll hit our stride today, Sankey." His old confidence came back as quickly as the cold disappeared. The horses broke into a trot, and the carriage clattered gaily around a corner.

"I'd like to get the melodeon in place early and —," Sankey said over the racket.

But D.L. edged forward in the seat. "This driver's cousin to Jehu. Watch it, Sankey. He's going to take this corner—." Around the corner, the carriage swung on two wheels. At the same moment, both D.L. and Sankey saw the melodeon shift and then begin to slide.

"Driver!" D.L. shouted in panic.

The carriage righted itself.

"Grab it! Grab it!" Sankey yelled.

"Driver, stop!"

But it was too late. When they jumped from the carriage, the melodeon lay half-shattered on the cobblestones. Numbly, D.L. and Sankey stared down at it.

That night D.L. faced his congregation alone. He saw some lean-jawed Scotsmen peer around curiously. "Friends, we had a bad accident this afternoon. So Sankey won't be here tonight. The meetings aren't the same without his brand of music but we'll get along somehow."

Yet in spite of the bad start and the kist fu' o' whistles, Edinburgh liked D.L. and big-voiced Sankey. They said D.L. told a Scotsman's kind of jokes. They said Sankey was as sincere as a bagpipe and, actually, not quite as loud!

For two weeks, D.L. preached his heart out in the

cramped nonconformist chapels. Then it happened. A leading Edinburgh minister made a public statement.

"On behalf of the clergy of the Church of Scotland in Edinburgh, I heartily endorse the two American lads and urge my congregation to attend their meetings. I may add, the professors of the Edinburgh University have done likewise."

"God bless them!" D.L. thought to himself as he sat over a cup of tea late at night. The meeting was over, Sankey had gone to his lodgings and Emma was asleep. Alone, D.L. nursed his tea and dreamed. It seemed as if this must be what he had prayed for. The Scotsmen had accepted him. He stirred his tea absently. What this meant he was not sure. It might mean that he would be able to preach in some of Edinburgh's big churches, after all. That means more crowds and that meant more men and women finding God. And that, after all, was what he was there for.

"When will they stop hearing my bad grammar and start seeing Jesus Christ in what I say," he had prayed not long ago. It looked as if the answer was on its way.

"Praise God," he thought. He could not have gone home to the United States like a whipped dog. And now? The tea was getting cold, but D.L. dreamed on. Maybe London, some day. How would it be to preach to ten thousand Londoners! Praise God that Edinburgh had accepted him!

The next few weeks in Edinburgh were better than anything he and Sankey had dreamed. The crowds packed the church. They sang and they listened. Then hundreds walked down the long aisles to find Christ in the after meetings. The biggest church in Edinburgh filled its galleries when he preached there.

The churchmen continued to be enthusiastic about what the Americans had done in Edinburgh. All over Scotland, they were talking about the Americans. England heard too. Horatius Bonar busily issued statements to curious reporters who came for facts.

"That's right," he would say. "I'd make this statement to any newspaper reporter. There's hardly a Christian household in Edinburgh where one or more people haven't been converted in the Moody meetings. Print that in your London paper. I'll stand right behind it."

But one day, Horatius Bonar walked into D.L.'s lodgings. Something was wrong. D.L. suggested a cup of hot tea at once. But Bonar, standing stiffly by the windows, said, "I think not, Mrs. Moody."

Emma fluttered a little. "It won't be any trouble, Dr. Bonar."

He shook his head. Then D.L. boomed, "Sit down, sir. Sit right down." But the Scotsman continued to stand by the window.

"I'll be up with the children if you want." Emma left in a hurry.

Well, D.L. wondered, is this a Scotch mood I have not seen before? "What's troubling you, Dr. Bonar?" he said out loud. "Roof cave in over at the cathedral?"

Bonar did not smile. "Mr. Moody, did you live in Chicago?"

"Sure I did."

"You were employed there?"

"That's right," D.L. began easily. "Before God made it clear that fortune-seeking was wr—."

111

"Employed by the C.N. Henderson Shoe Company?"

D.L. nodded. From his pocket, Bonar gravely took a letter, unfolded it with no haste and said, "Mr. Moody, this is written by a man who lives in Chicago. Tell me, did you ever work for any other shoe company there?"

Then D.L. explained how Henderson had died, how Buel, Hill, and Granger had hired him. He mentioned Wiswall too. When he finished, Bonar said, "That fits in with what I read here."

"Well, what do you read there?" D.L. blurted out uncomfortably.

"Something that could change the course of your evangelistic efforts." For a minute, Bonar watched silently the gray Edinburgh outside. "Mr. Moody, this letter says that when you were working for Henderson, you kept up your friendship with a rival company. That you were paid by the rival company for handing over to them valuable merchandising information!"

"Stuff and nonsense," D.L. said.

"I hope so, Mr. Moody." Horatius Bonar sat down in the easy chair, crumpling up his long legs uncomfortably. "But it isn't so simple. Unfortunately a copy of this letter is now in the hands of every minister in Edinburgh."

Chapter Fourteen

I GAVE WISWALL an honest day's work. When I left him, I gave Henderson full measure too. That letter is stuff and nonsense," D.L. said. But he knew that it was his word against the letter and that this was not going to be good enough.

"I'll fight it. Fight it hard. Call your committee together, Dr. Bonar—the committee that invited me here. That's where I'll start."

But his words were braver than his heart. When the Scotsman had left, D.L. sat alone. Why had this happened? It had taken the cool Scots so long to accept him. Now this. It could ruin his preaching here, and this was not the kind of business people kept to themselves.

When he faced the committee, he was ready for the fight. He reviewed for them his days as a shoe salesman in detail.

The chairman was kind. "Now, laddie, the committee takes your word for this matter. We give you our vote of confidence." But he went on. "Laddie, remember, Scotsmen are a cautious people, verra cautious with their money and verra cautious with their sentiment. When they think a man can't be trusted with money, they're just a wee bit more cautious with their sentiment. It's the others—all the ministers in this big city—that have this letter. They're the ones that worry us. Laddie, this has hurt you terribly, and there's nothing a vote of confidence from us can do about that." The old Scotsman crossed the room and rested his hand on D.L.'s shoulder. But D.L. was not comforted. He moved away.

He had planned his next step. "You're wrong. We can do something."

The old chairman looked concerned. "Now, laddie, you wouldn't want to get yourself into a verra great unpleasantness, would you?"

"It won't be my battle," D.L. said. "It'll be yours."

The committee buzzed unhappily.

"Don't take my word for my honesty. *Don't* give

113

me a vote of confidence." D.L. walloped the top of a bookcase. "Go to the root of things. Write to Chicago. Tell everybody that you are investigating."

"Investigating?" The committee clucked in distress. "Now, laddie."

"Sure. Ask about me. Ask about D.L. Moody's business dealings, from start to finish. Ask if he's honest. When you get the answer, make it public. Like this fellow made his lies."

It took more punching of the bookcase to convince them. They protested that this was not the Scottish way. But D.L. outtalked all objections.

One final question remained. "While we're waiting for the answer to our investigation, laddie, and the committee is not giving you a vote of confidence and the other clergy in town are holding onto their copies of the letter—well, laddie, what will happen to your meetings?"

He was ready for this too. "They'll go right on." The Scotsmen looked uneasy, but D.L. said, "If God wants to use me He'll send folks to the meetings. I'll keep on preaching.

They wrote the letter that week. D.L. went on preaching, and Sankey singing, six nights a week. There was gossip, but the Edinburgh people came to hear the Americans. After every meeting, the inquiry rooms were full.

But there were murmurs on the fringes, and the wait for the verification from Chicago was endless. The murmurings could grow into shouts if they went on unchecked.

Then Horatius Bonar came to D.L.'s lodgings again. "Mr. Moody, I have a letter here."

"Good news from Chicago?"

"You heard too?"

"Nope," D.L. said calmly. "I prayed." And it was exactly what he had expected.

> We, the undersigned, pastors of Chicago, learning that the Christian character of D.L. Moody has been attacked, do not hesitate to recommend him as an earnest Christian worker worthy of the confidence of our Scotch brethren with whom he is now laboring, believing that the Master will be honored by them in so receiving him among them as a co-laborer in the vineyard of the Lord.

"Praise the Lord!" D.L. said. "It pays to fight."
The little gossipings had been extinguished. So Edinburgh people went on singing Sankey's songs, more lustily than ever. And D.L. went on preaching to the crowds.

From Edinburgh, they were invited to Glasgow There not a church or a hall in the city was big enough to hold the crowds. And some people walked thirty miles to the meetings.

What was happening was like nothing that D.L. had ever dreamed—or even prayed for. Yet he was canny enough—and honest enough—to know that there were still a good many churchmen in Great Britain who wished that he had stayed at home. This was in his mind when he talked with a man named Hugh Matheson who had come to Scotland from London to ask him a favor.

"Mr. Moody, London is a big, dirty city with an abundance of sin. It needs your kind of preaching. Will you come to London?"

What was it he had said to Emma when they first landed? He had said it again when the going had been so rough. "If I could only preach in London, Emma." London would be the ultimate.

He said frankly to Matheson, "It's always been my dream, Mr. Matheson. I've prayed about it.

And thought about what I'd say if somebody asked me. I'm being honest."

Matheson sipped his tea appreciatively and beamed. "Mr. Moody, this is quite an answer to prayer itself. We can talk about dates right away."

"Hold on there," D.L. set his own teacup down firmly. "I never said that. Hear me out. The fact is, I won't come."

Matheson's cup rattled in the saucer.

"That's where my praying and thinking took me. I won't come to London, Matheson. Not unless I get some things the way I want them."

"I'm sure that we can arrange——."

"Whom do you represent?" D.L. interrupted.

"Some Christian businessmen, sir, who have a burden for Londoners——."

"Not good enough."

"And our pastors——."

"Nope. Mr. Matheson, here's my condition. I won't come to London until I get invited by every minister in the city. I know what I'm saying. I battled opposition all over these islands. But London is too big to fight single-handed. I need co-operation and I want organization and you got to get that through channels." He sat back and looked sternly at Matheson. He knew what he wanted and he was not going to touch London with a ten-foot pole unless he got it.

So Hugh Matheson went back sadly to London. D.L. went on to Glasgow where three thousand joined the church and seventy thousand wrote their names on small cards to say that they acknowledged Jesus Christ as their Saviour.

D.L. put London out of his mind. He and Sankey traveled on to Forfar, Aberdeen, Tain, and Huntley.

At Huntley, he spoke to fifteen thousand at once in the open air.

They were invited to Ireland. He spoke in Belfast, Londonderry, and Dublin. At Dublin, he had a visitor. "Mr. Moody, you can't brush me off. I've traveled all these miles." It was Hugh Matheson again, plaintive and coaxing.

But D.L. was tired and busy. "Well, what are you waiting for, Matheson?"

The Londoner fumbled in his vest pocket. "Mr. Moody, this is an important document. A petition." He began to read. " 'It is hereby determined to arrange special evangelistic work in London next year and agreed that a fund of not less than ten thousand pounds—ten thousand, Mr. Moody—.' "

D.L. digested the number. "That sounds like a nice round figure. It ought to pay for considerable organization. Go on."

"And—uh—'that this fund be placed in the hands of the treasurer and that men of distinguished evangelistic gifts in the work be invited not only from other parts of England, but also from America, Scotland, and Ireland to assist in the movement.' Well? What do you think?"

"I think any kind of evangelistic work is a mighty good sign. But I don't know why I'm supposed to think anything special. I didn't hear my name read off." With amusement, D.L. watched for Matheson's reaction.

"Mr. Moody! This is a petition signed by a group of men who represent all the ministers in London. All of them want Moody and Sankey there."

D.L. chuckled. "Why didn't you say so? That's great news. Fine and dandy."

"Your answer?"

117

"Yes. A thousand times yes. It's all I was waiting for. It's all settled. I'll come."

Yet, when he thought it over, he knew he was not quite ready to go to London. He had to be sure that the Londoners understood him. He did not want any embarrassment to discredit all his preaching so far. So he made one more stipulation: a personal conference with the London ministers.

The conference was called; D.L. traveled cross country to reach it. More than five hundred London clergymen waited for him. D.L. faced them from the platform, as informal as if he were selling shoes, as eloquent as if he were talking about Hell to pagans.

He said directly, "Gentlemen, I asked my friend, Hugh Matheson to herd all you ministers in here. I want to get some things straight before I preach in your city. I expect you've heard some strange things about me."

A titter ran through the crowd.

"So I'm not here today to contradict a thing. I want you to talk about what you've heard. Questions from the floor, please."

There were thirty seconds of silence.

"I don't care how we get insulted. You ask them."

A fat man stood up in the fifth row. "Mr. Moody, are you hired by P. T. Barnum?"

Again, the titter. D.L. walked to the front of the platform, leaned over. "Why, sir, P. T. Barnum wouldn't want me. But if I keep on gaining weight on English beef, he might put me in his side show. Next question."

From somewhere in the back, a husky voice called, "Is Mr. Sankey peddling American organs?"

D.L. grinned. "If he is, he's doing a bad job. Hasn't sold one. All right, that man back there is next."

"Mr. Moody, we've heard some serious accusations about what you do with the funds from the collections. Also, the royalties on the little hymnbooks."

D.L. stepped from the edge of the platform, paced to the rostrum, passed it, paced to the other side of the platform. Questions about the hymnbooks upset him. The hymnbook that he and Sankey had compiled since they had come to Great Britain had sold well. But they had published it so that more people could sing the Gospel, not to buy their wives fine furs.

"I don't keep a penny of the royalties. Neither does Sankey. It all goes back to the United States to build up a church that was burned to the ground awhile back. As for the other question! Mr. Matheson, you're treasurer of the London committee. Right now, I give over to you all the collections taken at the London meetings."

Now men jumped up all over the auditorium. "Will everybody's church get a fair share of the converts?"

"That's a good question," he said shortly. "But it isn't mine. My job is bringing them to Christ, not packing the membership lists of you London ministers."

"Do you honestly intend to do anything about London's miserably poor?"

"Sure. And I'll tell you something else. I'll do something about London's miserably rich too."

They laughed again, but he felt the difference. They were on his side. "Time for one more."

A man in the left section. "Mr. Moody, I'm no heresy hunter. But we'd all feel better if we had your creed. Can you get it published before the campaign?"

D.L. paced to the edge of the platform, bent down

and spoke confidentially. "No need to. It's already in print." He paused. "You'll find it in black and white—in Isaiah 53!"

He held up his hand. "I guess London is ready for Moody. But I'll admit something. Moody ain't ready for London. He won't ever be. But God is. He'll stand up there in Moody's shoes."

Chapter Fifteen

SO D.L. WENT TÓ LONDON. The biggest city in the world was a long way from the Connecticut River Valley and the Court Street shoestore. The Royal Opera House in London's West End was remote also from the pinched second-floor over George Bennett's York apothecary.

In London D.L. preached in four great halls—Agricultural Hall, the Royal Opera House, Camberwell Hall, and in the East End, an auditorium built especially for him. It seated ten thousand. Three or four times a day he preached and Sankey sang. They kept up this pace for four months. Altogether, they held more than 285 meetings and talked to an estimated audience of two million Englishmen.

"Just think," D.L. would chuckle. "D.L. Moody, ex-shoe salesman from America who says *ain't* and who's getting too fat for his suits. Well, well! 'The world has yet to see what God can do with one man wholly committed to Him.'"

Then he had to leave it all. In 1875, he and Emma, Sankey and Fanny started home. But now the whole world looked different. And it *was* different. He had sailed away from New York as an unsponsored, free-lance religious worker. Three years later, he was coming home as a world-famous evangelist.

Home now meant the farm in Northfield; the house destroyed by the Chicago fire had never been replaced. From New York, he and Emma took a train directly to Northfield. As it smoked through the Massachusetts villages, he thought about the farm and the valley with affection.

Before he had seen the world, the valley had been ugly. Before he knew that he had the wings to fly over the hills, they were prison walls. Now they were as beautiful as the British lake country. And there was nothing to compare in flat Indiana and Illinois. These hills were home. He peered out of the window for signs of Northfield.

When the train pulled in, there was a crowd on the station platform. A hundred townspeople had come to welcome him. Climbing out of the train, he remembered the day he had boarded it—with five dollars belonging to his big brother.

"Welcome home, Mr. Moody."

"You're a credit to the valley, son."

"Always did say you'd amount to something. In spite of your tomfoolery."

He shook hands with them, gave God and Emma all the credit, remembered more names than he thought he could. He walked through the station, joking, repeating how good it was to come home.

"Well, Dwight, now that you're famous, and got your name in the Boston papers, what are you going to do about it?"

It was one remark in a hundred that night but it stuck. All the way to the farm in the carriage with Emma, he could not dislodge the memory of it. Later that night, when all the first hellos had been

121

said—to his mother, young Sam and the rest of his brothers still living there in the town—he sat at the bedroom window, looking at the hills, thinking about that question.

Being famous was one thing. Handling fame—and the influence that went with it—was another. What was he going to do now? He had no job. Again he was trusting God for everything. But now he had a family to take care of—Emma, little Emma, and Will.

He looked out at the hills, so smooth and curved that God might have carved them with His hand and gently slipped them into place. All one piece, all fitting together. This is the way it had to be with a man's life too. "Well, Dwight, now that you're famous, what are you going to do about it?"

Then he remembered. *The world has yet to see what God can do with one man wholly committed to Him.*

The problem would not be solved in a day. The mail that week exaggerated it. Every day there were invitations from American ministers to preach in their churches. And the August weather was a distraction. D.L. resisted his mail and instead went for long rides with Sam, his younger brother.

One day, they turned off the main road and leisurely bounced along the uphill, back-country roads. D.L. settled back in the carriage seat. "Sam, I've been dreaming of that view of the Connecticut River for years. This is God's country, Sam.

"Uh-huh," Sam said absently, flicking the horse with his whip. "Maybe you're right. I'm too close to it, I guess. The valley's home to me, and that's that."

D.L. raised his voice to preach to the pines. "Man's a lucky man to live here. Right back here in the hills. Yes, sir. Why, looking at that view is enough to convince a man there's a God."

Sam shrugged. "Don't know. There's one that might not agree with you." He pointed the whip toward a shack in the pines.

D.L. jerked around. "Who's that?"

"Fellow that lives there. Paralyzed from the neck down. He never sees the valley."

"Stop the wagon!"

"What?"

"I want to talk to that man." Sam reined up the horses. "That's his wife on the steps?"

"Young ones are his daughters. You can see them there all the time in good weather. They're braiding straw. Making hats to sell. That's how the family lives. Look here, Dwight, are you sure—?"

"Wait here." D.L. was out of the wagon. Young girls were imprisoned back here in the hills. No chance for education. The village school was too far. Naturally they had no money to pay, anyway. The tight closed-in-ness he knew when he was their age smothered him. Were they bright? What if they had a chance?

Ten minutes' talk convinced him. The girls were Yankee-smart. The mother was bright, too, but bitter. Sam had been wrong about the father. Paralyzed, he had a humble invincible faith in God and a trust in his salvation through Jesus Christ. And they all loved their valley.

Back in the wagon, D.L. grunted to Sam to start for home. He had raced into the shack sure that here were people who needed to be converted. Instead he found a family sensitive to Jesus Christ in the middle of a terrible life. Two bright girls, doomed to braid hats to support a father who might live for twenty years!

123

"Sam, I got a crazy idea. Maybe God wants me to do something for that man. Or those two girls. And all the rest like them up here. So He sent me nosing around back here."

Sam was puzzled. "You mean, start a church up here?"

But D.L. was not thinking of a church. Why not give bright minds a chance for a Christian education? "I mean a school. I mean start a school."

Sam looked over at his brother affectionately. "Don't let your pity run away with your common sense. You're a preacher. You're a *famous* preacher."

"Maybe that's my claim."

"Huh?" Sam shook his head, mystified.

"Maybe that gives me a chance to start a school that some others don't have. I sure can't lay claim to much education for myself." He watched the rounded complete line of hills against sky. "I got friends. I got influence. Maybe that's what gets a school built."

"But *why?* Dwight, you better let this dream go before you do anything rash."

He said nothing more. But inside, the dream simmered. Help others to climb over those hills and then come back again the way he had—to help others. He could do it through education—Christian education. As he dreamed, the carriage jolted along under the elms on Main Street and turned left to the Moody farm.

But the mail could no longer be ignored. The next day Emma faced him in the farm dining room with an ominous sheaf of letters. "D.L., I'm at my wit's end keeping up with your mail. If you'd just sit still long enough to tell me how to answer some of these."

D.L. pulled back the heavy oak chair and dropped

124

into it. "All right," he said good-naturedly. "I'll sit. What do you want to know?"

"Brooklyn wrote again."

"Oh, oh."

"They want an answer. They have an option to rent a rink. It seats six thousand people. They have to know."

"A rink? Don't like the sound of it. Don't know as I like Brooklyn, either. Preached there once before. Cold place."

"D.L., you can't toss it off like this."

Then he leaned across the table and took the letters from her hand. He laid the letters on the table and covered them with one of his hands. "Emma," he said very quietly. "You and me, we're the same people but in a way we aren't. Everything's different now. We saw what happened in England. This is more than saying yes to a man in Brooklyn. There'll be other places. Am I going to let people flatter me into hopping from one place to another?"

"But you're going to Brooklyn to preach," she said.

"Or am I going to stay in one place? Stay there and do something worth while for God."

"You mean Chicago, don't you?" she said very quietly. "You want to go back."

Then he told her. It was Northfield he had in mind. He sketched his idea for a school to give a Christian education to girls who could not buy any education.

But Emma looked confused. "A school, D.L.? You? Why, you didn't—." she stopped.

He knew what she meant. "But I *married* a schoolteacher, Emma," he reminded her. "I could build a school."

She said nothing, looking down at the pile of

letters under his hand. Finally, he looked down at them too, and after awhile picked up one and read it. He read the plea from the Brooklyn people and then he read the letter they had written before that one. As he sat there at the table, he knew that these voices were too loud. By sheer force, they were drowning out his dream.

Was that what God wanted? D.L. Moody hopping from city to city, doing what he liked to do best. He sighed and put down the letters again. He would say yes to Brooklyn.

Two months later, October, 1875, he was in Brooklyn, preaching in the rented rink to six thousand a day. Sankey was there too. The people sang and sang to the little melodeon. And when D.L. invited them, hundreds walked down the aisles into the inquiry rooms.

What was to come after Brooklyn remained a question. What did God want? One day two visitors came to his temporary office in the Brooklyn rink and tried to make up his mind. George Stuart and his friend were Philadelphia businessmen and, when D.L. learned they were good friends of John Wanamaker, he lifted piles of hymnbooks and old papers from chairs and made room for them to sit down.

They came directly to the point. Would D.L. preach in Philadelphia? The firm, set smiles on their faces showed they did not expect no for an answer. It was useless to try to explain his problem. They took it for granted that he was about to launch a gigantic speaking circuit that would not end until he had conducted his unique campaigns in most major cities in the United States. There was no question in their minds that this was what God wanted too.

They were so sure. He found himself thinking

126

out loud to the two strangers. "Preaching to crowds is meat and drink to me. Can't deny it. Would it be like that if God didn't want to keep me up there before the crowds? Convincing men, persuading them —it's always been the big reward. First it was shoes and now it's the Gospel." He was not really talking to Stuart and his friend. "When you see that red-headed man over there start down the aisle—a little blond girl from the balcony—that grandmother over there—a hundred of them coming to Jesus Christ because you spoke the words—why, there ain't nothing else like it in the world." He was answering the question for himself. "Yes, I'll come to Philadelphia. But on one condition."

The two men smiled broadly at each other. "What's your condition?"

"I respect men who think big. I like big halls and crowds and meetings. Sloppiness and confusion send me crazy. So you get yourself organized down there in Philadelphia and get me a hall that's big enough for a crowd. I want to see about double what we packed in here in Brooklyn. Rent me a hall that's big enough to hold an army of sinners. Then I'll come to Philadelphia."

But the condition he had imposed was not a simple one. Going home on the train, the two Philadelphians thought they had the answer. "Rent the biggest barn in Philly. The Pennsylvania freight depot." The depot was in the middle of the city; it had just been put up for sale and it was not being used for freight or storage. It would seat more than ten thousand, enough for Moody.

The Pennsylvania Railroad officials disappointed them. A Philadelphia businessman had placed an option on the depot, and the railroad could not rent it. Under pressure, the railroad dug into its files, releasing the name of the man who wanted to buy. It was John Wanamaker.

At first, Stuart was elated. Almost immediately, he was downcast. Wanamaker was in Europe. Then he cabled him.

> John Wanamaker: Have booked Moody for Philadelphia campaign. Desperately need large hall. Only Pennsylvania freight depot satisfactory. Officials refuse to rent, pending your decision to buy. Will you cancel option?
> (Signed) George Stuart.

They waited for the answer. It came.

> George Stuart: No intention of changing mind re: Pennsylvania freight depot. Building and location needed for future business expansion. Returning home shortly.
> (Signed) John Wanamaker.

Impatiently, the committee of Philadelphians who had invited D.L. to their city waited for Wanamaker's return. Their only chance was personal debate with him. Somewhat crossly, they greeted him when he arrived back at his office. "You're blocking the campaign."

"Now, gentlemen, remember, I'm a Christian businessman," Wanamaker countered. "Businessman—and Christian. I need the depot. So I buy it. Nothing wrong with that. Papers are signed already. Then I christen it the best way I know how. I let D.L. Moody do it." He looked around triumphantly. "Got a surprise for the committee. It would break my heart to let you good men pay your money for rent. So I finished buying it just so you don't have to. It's all yours and Moody's for as long as he'll stay. Rent free!"

When D.L. arrived in Philadelphia, he saw that preparations had been handled in the business-like way he admired. John Wanamaker himself arranged for the seating. He ordered 8,900 chairs for the main floor, 1,300 for the balcony. Then he ordered eight more.

"Eight more?" D.L. was puzzled.

"Eight chairs don't seem like much. But they can make the difference between half a house—and two thousand folks turned away the first night."

D.L. still didn't understand.

"Nobody looks at round numbers. But they take notice of exact ones. Now the hall holds 10,208. Good business sense, D.L."

This was the kind of business sense that had sold shoes for D.L. Moody, traveling salesman for C. N. Henderson. It worked in Philadelphia too. There he preached to about twice the Brooklyn crowd, 10,208 seats were full almost every night. Every morning, he held an eight o'clock service, and the lines for this began to form in front of the Depot Tabernacle at 4:30 A.M.

While in Philadelphia, D.L. was invited to New York City. He accepted. In New York that spring, he packed the pride of Madison Avenue, the glittery, glamorous, brand-new Hippodrome. He was caught up and carried along by the thrill of the crowds and the emotion of the inquiry rooms.

The world has yet to see what God can do with one man wholly committed to Him. Every day, D.L. marveled at what God was doing with the boy from the valley farm.

In New York he saw an old Chicago friend, an energetic schoolteacher from what had been his Illinois Street Church and was now the Chicago Avenue Church. Emeline Dryer had come all the way to New York for a personal conference with D.L. She wanted his approval for a pet project of hers because, as she told him, his word still carried a lot of weight at the church he had begun in the North Market Dance Hall.

As D.L. stacked up hymnbooks, she told her story. For several years, she had been conducting some serious-minded Bible study classes at the church, and they were growing. But because the city was so big and people were so scattered, it was only practical to hold classes once a week. Yet folks needed, and wanted, more instruction than that.

"Now here's my idea. I want your permission to raise the money to buy up a house near the church. My Bible students could live together here and be handy for evening classes."

D.L. deposited the hymnbooks on a chair. "Don't sound practical to me, Emeline. Not at all. I can't approve of some hairbrained scheme like that."

Her eyes snapped. "It isn't hairbrained. I have a place in mind. It's a real brick dump but it's cheap and it's next to the Chicago Avenue Church. It would do."

"No, a thousand times no."

"Mr. Moody, I came from Chicago to get your approval."

"No! A thousand times no! I have no intentions of standing off here in New York City and approving something I know so little about. But I'll think it over, Emeline. Then one of these days I'll come out to Chicago and we can talk some more about it."

He moved off with more hymnbooks. Such an intense little woman—intelligent, educated enough to be college dean, dedicated enough to go on for years teaching her Bible classes. But her scheme was not business-like. Such a strange idea! Then, for no apparent reason, unless perhaps it was Emeline Dryer's bright eyes, he was reminded of two country girls braiding hats on the Northfield back road.

Chapter Sixteen

D L., THIS IDEA OF YOURS about a school is as practical as starting a ship-building academy in the White Mountains. These forsaken hills are no place for a young ladies' finishing school." That was what D.L.'s friend, Marshall, had told him candidly earlier that morning. It was a brisk fall day, 1878, and the two men were in front of the Moody farm, out by the road, looking over the valley.

All morning, D.L. had been talking as vigorously as if he were preaching in the Hippodrome. Forsaken hills, huh? With drama, he told about the two bright girls doomed to braid hats for a lifetime, unless somebody made an education possible. They could not afford to pay for what the village offered, and besides the village offered very little for girls. There were dozens more like those two bright Yankees—in farmhouses, in hill shacks, throughout the "forsaken hills."

As for a finishing school! Irritatedly D.L. scorned that. He had in mind practical basic education with no frills—a Christian education centered about the Bible, giving Christ and the Word of God first place. Finishing school! "I guess not," D.L. declared.

Now—and it was nearly noon—the well-to-do Boston businessman seemed almost convinced. It never occurred to D.L. that he might just be tired. "Come around here," D.L. demanded. "Look beyond that fence. There now. Squint your eyes. Think about a gray stone hall, right over there where the elm is."

"Ummm," Marshall said unenthusiastically.

"What would you see from the windows?" D.L. persisted.

"The river, I suppose. Lots of trees. The valley."

Was the man blind? What spread out before him was one of the most exciting scenes in the country. Looking away to the hills, D.L. remembered city streets he had walked along, rivers he had crossed, towns he had ridden through since he had come back from England. The first year, Brooklyn, Philadelphia, New York. The year after that, Chicago, Boston. The third year—the winter of 1877-78—a circuit of small eastern cities, Springfield, Massachusetts, Hartford and New Haven, Connecticut. Now he had come back to rest in the valley.

"You'd see God's creation from those windows, Marshall. That's Christian education too. Who can doubt there's a God who wrote the plan of salvation, looking at that!"

Marshall was not unenthusiastic but he was convinced. He admitted that D.L. knew the country, its needs, and potential. He looked again at the pasture land. "All right," he said. "If you can buy up that seedy looking pasture, I'll see that you get some money. That's what you wanted me to say, wasn't it, you old schemer?"

They were still there talking about it, D.L. sketching out the building he had in mind, when a wagon clacked alongside. The driver called out a casual good morning, added an offhand comment about an early frost and was clattering off when D.L. jumped into action. Would the man like to meet his Boston friend? Emma had just been asking about his wife's health. Maybe he would like to come to the house for a spell.

But the Northfield farmer was shy. He backed away when he heard that Marshall was a Boston man. D.L. was in front of the wagon now, hand on the horse, talking fast. Reluctantly, the farmer lumbered from the wagon.

"This is the man that owns the pasture!" Clapping the farmer on the back, he said, "I think you'd like to sell."

The farmer squared his jaw. "I didn't come here to sell you nothing, Mr. Moody."

Marshall smiled to himself and looked away. D.L. prodded the farmer up toward the pasture. "That don't make any difference. Will you sell?"

Marshall, tagging along behind, spoke up. "I think it's pretty plain your friend wants to retain his rights."

"It ain't that. That land is nothing but corn and stubble. Mr. Moody's a friend of mine. I don't want him to get hurt."

"I see the stubble," D.L. said.

The farmer turned to Marshall. "Sir, Mr. Moody, he's a good man but he don't know land. He's been in the city too long."

Marshall smiled. D.L. raised his voice. "I want that land. You let me worry about the stubble." A chance like this would not happen again in ten years—the man with the land and the man with the money standing there together in the middle of his dream. "It'll be on my conscience. All the stone and stubble."

"Well—," the farmer said, wiping his hand diffidently on his overalls.

"Come into the house, and we'll talk business details." D.L. headed the farmer toward the farmhouse. All the way, he looked back at his land sadly. "An awful lot of sand hills beyond the elms."

But the rest was merely a formality. Emma drew up some papers. The terms were made agreeable to all. The signatures went down. The hopelessly stubbly pasture was his to transform to a young ladies' finishing school!

This was the first purchase. There were others.

"Mr. Moody, you're balmy as a spring day if you want to buy up my land. I been cussing at every square inch for twenty years. Only worse land is what's next to it." The land next to it was, of course, the pasture that D.L. now owned.

One after another, D.L. bought up a ring of worthless, barren farms. Friends like Marshall gave the money although they gave it dubiously. Within six months, by the spring of 1879, it looked as if his long dream were coming true. How excited Sam would have been about it! But Sam had been dead two years.

One spring day, D.L. laid the cornerstone with his father's trowel. Construction started on classrooms and dormitory. Every day he walked out to the pasture to push the workmen like a campaign committee. "Fine and dandy, men. Keep it up. We got a schedule to meet."

But almost from the start, construction fell behind schedule. Workmen were as slow as Vermont molasses in January, he grumbled—won't ever be finished by November. And he had promised the girls. Announced it all over the countryside. Said they would have a school by November and everything would be all set up to begin classes then.

A hot summer came on, and the work slowed down. Nobody else worried. Emma was preoccupied with the new baby, Paul, born in the spring about the time the cornerstone was laid.

"D.L., is that you? Bring me a towel. I'm bathing the baby."

Coming in from his daily check on construction, he hardly heard her.

"Towel, D.L."

"The towels can wait," he said shortly. "I'm going upstairs to measure something. I think we got room right here in our own house. With a wall knocked out here and there," he added. "I figure we can turn the upstairs into a dormitory in no time at all. The dining room will do for classes. Temporary, so they won't mind crowding."

"What on earth are you talking about?"

Happily, he told her his plan to keep his promise about November classes: their own house could substitute for classrooms and dormitory too.

But Emma reminded him that he had a teen-aged daughter and a growing son. There was also a new baby in the house. Did he want to rip apart their home and fill it up with girls from the hills?

The carpenters descended on the Moody farm with hammers that made more noise than August thunder. The sawdust smelled like a picnic in the pine woods, but when Will and little Emma played too close to it, they sneezed all day. The baby learned how to outscream the racket for attention. The workmen crushed down the flower beds, and Emma was not too happy.

But toward the end of the summer, D.L. heard Emma ask the workmen for the measurements of the new windows in the upstairs dormitory room.

"I thought—well—I saw some pretty material down at the general store," she admitted to D.L. "I was thinking—D.L., those girls would appreciate some nice curtains, don't you think?"

As he predicted, the gray stone hall in the stubbly pasture was not finished by November. But the farmhouse dormitory was. Although D.L. and Emma were at a meeting in St. Louis, the school opened on time. Arriving for the first classes held in the

135

Moody dining room were three times as many girls as anybody had expected. More than twenty-five Northfield girls wanted a Christian education.

Later in the fall, D.L. came back to Northfield. For a long while, he stood in the back of a class, taught by one of the best teachers he could find. "The knack of persuading men, the talent for making fine friends with money to give away, the ability to know my own weaknesses—thank You for what You have given me, God," he mused. "I've tried to give them back to You, to commit them to You." How else could a country boy who skipped out of a one-room schoolhouse build up his own school?

He left the classroom then and went to stand on his front lawn. A mist covered the hills that blocked the green corridor made by the river. The mist made the valley seem infinite, without limits, big enough to contain the whole world.

Later that week, the valley did contain a visitor from Boston. Hiram Camp, slim and muscular for his seventy years, paced the Moody living room while D.L. lounged on the overstuffed couch. "Hiram, you came to the wrong man. I'm no good at legal matters."

"Making my will isn't a legal matter. I want spiritual help. That's why I came to you. I want to leave my money so that my death'll benefit the Christian community in some way."

D.L. considered the old man carefully. He must be skillful with his influence. Camp would be dead in another ten years. "Here's my advice to you. A man works hard to get his money. He's entitled to some fun while he's alive."

"But, Moody, you don't mean—."

D.L. hurried on. "Maybe not fun. Joy. Satisfaction.

Hiram, I recommend you give away that money before you die."

"But I was thinking of some kind of a monument, I guess."

"Then build it before you die," D.L. chirped. "Hiram, folks have been after me all fall to take boys in my school here. Up and down the valley, they come and tell me the same story. They tell me I'm cheating the boys. There's your monument, Hiram. Use your money. Build a school for boys like my Northfield."

"I'm too old."

"That's not true."

"It is." Hiram whirled. Cagily, he said, "If you think a boys' school is so important, build it yourself."

"All right, I will."

Hiram snorted. "You talked yourself right into that."

"I will—if you give me the money."

"Why, I—you—!" Hiram sputtered. Then he laughed. "All right. You win. Wait till I find my checkbook. Uh—." He pulled it from his pocket. "Here she is. Now then." He bent over the parlor table. "You're a shrewd one." The pen scratched across the check. "Here's my check for enough to buy a couple hundred acres and a few farmhouses. How's that?"

D.L. reached out and, before he touched the check, he saw that it read twenty-five thousand dollars.

"Go build your boys' school," Hiram Camp said.

"I intend to." D.L. kept his word. In May, 1881, Mount Hermon School opened officially in two Northfield farmhouses. Its purpose: to provide a Christian education for country boys who could not afford to pay their own way.

137

Chapter Seventeen

IT WAS FINE AND DANDY to be back in Chicago
again. He liked the smell of the city. It smelled as
if somebody had taken good shoe leather and mixed
it with rich black dirt. But he knew it was not that.
It was actually all the things contained in this young
lusty place—factory smoke, sawdust from houses being built, and stockyards.

It was great to be back in Chicago again and see
what fifteen years had done to the city that was so
bent on bigness that when it had a fire, it was a
fire big enough to eat out its own heart. Part of his
heart had stayed in Chicago, there in what was now
a grand place called the Chicago Avenue Church
but had started as a rag-tag bundle of slum kids
meeting in the North Market Hall for Sunday school
classes.

Yet D.L. was not enjoying his quick carriage ride
through Chicago streets on his stopover before he
caught a train south. At his side, there was a clip-
voiced, wiry little woman who pointed out distressing
things he wanted to overlook.

The woman was Emeline Dryer. She spoke in-
tensely. "On your right, Mr. Moody, that old warehouse. We rent it for almost nothing. We meet
downstairs for classes. Upstairs we have a good-
sized dormitory."

D.L. grunted. "Looks as if it ought to be condemned."

"I suppose it should," Emeline said patiently. "But
actually, the old buildings are more satisfactory than
the tents—for our purposes."

"Some day that'll topple over. Emeline, I've seen enough. I figure it's time to head for my train. You showed me enough old wrecks all over the city to give me a good picture of what goes on here. And if I'd known this is what it would amount to, I'd never have given my approval back in '76."

In 1876, after D.L. had rebuffed Emeline at their Hippodrome meeting, she had not let the matter drop. She waited until he came to preach in Chicago later that year. She had approached him again with new arguments for giving folks a place to live together for more convenient evening Bible classes. Hesitantly, D.L. had approved the project. Since then, Emeline and her supporters had gathered together bands of earnest Bible students in third-rate living quarters all over the city.

"It looks like a crazy gypsy outfit too poor to live like decent folks. What kind of testimony is that, Emeline?" It hurt him because he always wanted Christianity to think as big as business. Farwell Hall was a big structure. The Illinois Street Church had been well-constructed. He never preached in shacks or rundown tents; such places did not honor the Gospel of Christ. He was discouraged by what he had seen and sorry that, in some way, he was responsible for it.

But as the carriage headed toward the Loop, Emeline kept talking. "We know what you say is right, Mr. Moody. That's why we want you to help us with our next step. We think that if we can take the little knots of people scattered all over the city now and organize them—."

"Organize them!" He snorted. "Into what?"

The carriage rolled on. "We aren't sure. Some kind of a school. A school to train adults, men and women church members—."

D.L. interrupted. "Organize them. All you'd have would be organized condemned warehouses and blown-down tents and mixed-up people. No, sir, Emeline. I'm surprised at you. Now I know why you want me to talk to your friends tonight."

"That's right. That's why—."

"—why you took me on this ride. To raise my sympathy. Well, you got it. So much sympathy that I'm going to be cold and practical. Here's what I'll say tonight. Don't consider organizing this motley crowd of people and buildings until you can collect a financial backlog of $250,000!"

Emeline blanched, holding on to the side of the carriage as they rounded a corner.

"You can't budget with a penny less. When you get that, let me know. Then I might be interested in talking school to you."

The carriage took them back to the Loop. D.L., glancing sideways at the bright little woman, knew that she was not finished either with him or her pet project. He clucked to himself over her determination and then turned to look out the carriage windows. He recalled a young fellow who used to sell shoes that way—up and down the same Chicago streets.

From Chicago, he went south, and the winter of 1885-86 was as busy as all the rest. He preached in the South and then returned to campaign in the North. Six months later he was back—back in Chicago, booked for four months of meetings.

Six nights a week he filled churches, the new Farwell Hall, and the hugest roller-skating rinks in the city. "They're all coming to hear Crazy Moody, who can't pronounce Jerusalem any clearer than ever," he would laugh to Emma. *The world has*

140

yet to see what God can do with one man wholly committed to Him.

This was his mood on January 22, 1886, before he preached. He understood so well now the power of his influence. Six months before, he had named $250,000 to Emeline Dryer and her friends. Now they informed him: "We've raised it all. We're looking for your help."

In that spirit, he went before the crowded hall. That night in his sermon, he said: "The ministers are up here and the common folk are down there and there's a kind of gap between them. Now there aren't enough ministers to do all the things the church needs done. What can we do about it? We have to get gap men. That's right, gap men to stand between the people and the ministers. Who are the gap men? Why, they're the common folk, like you and me."

And Emeline Dryer seized on this too. "You said the church needs gap men. If we organize all the Bible study classes, that's what we'll have. A school to train gap men."

D.L. heard her sympathetically, knowing that the financial backlog had been collected. Yet he promised nothing actually. And his mind was still on his first responsibility, the preaching mission to Chicago. He pushed Emeline's school to the back of his mind and went on preaching every night. Four months passed.

"God has blessed these four months. Now I hate to close up the campaign. Keep up the good work. You've started the city talking about Jesus Christ," he exhorted the people. "Don't let it down now. In these last minutes, I'll put it up to you. Will you carry on after I'm gone?"

As usual, the audience was swept along by the

color and rhythm of his words. From the back some-body shouted, "Yes. Amen. We will."

D.L. bounced around the pulpit. "I got an answer. Praise the Lord! All right, back there, how are you going to carry on what you started here?"

Somebody stood up. "Hire a big tent. Hold meetings straight through the summer."

D.L. slapped the pulpit. "There's a man after my own heart. 'Hire a big tent,' he says. All right, sir, you do it." The congregation smiled appreciatively, uneasily. "And here's the first hundred dollars for rent, right up here beside the Bible. It's my gift."

Before D.L. left the city, he heard the plan for continuing. They would hire a tent and bring in an evangelist or several evangelists to speak. It would all be organized as D.L. himself organized his campaigns. There would be inquiry rooms and special helpers for the after-meetings. The helpers would be laymen but they would be trained laymen.

D.L. did not need to ask where they would be trained. It all fitted together like a puzzle. The trained laymen would be the men and women who had studied the Bible in condemned warehouses and frowsy tents.

What happened next was inevitable. The organization of the Bible classes was born and named the Chicago Evangelization Society. D.L. rolled the name over on his tongue. It had a sound as solid as a business firm but it also witnessed to its faith. D.L. gave his blessing to the loose network of Bible study classes straggled out across the city.

Back East, he got reports that the organization served its purpose. In the spring of '87, it brought all the students together for a concentrated institute.

In the spring of '88, they also met together for several days of intensive study.

In 1889, D.L. was invited to teach at the Chicago Evangelization Society's annual spring institute. The enrollment was six times what he expected.

"I'm happy as a clam at high tide about this," he told his classes. "This kind of changes my mind about a lot of things and I'll admit it."

At last he felt that a school for the purpose of indoctrinating in vital churchmanship would succeed. "This means," he joked with Chicago Evangelization Society leaders, "I'm willing to throw my whole weight behind your scheme—all 280 pounds of it."

The next day he walked with Emeline Dryer out to survey the Chicago Avenue Church neighborhood. He looked at the building which she had described to him in 1876 at the Hippodrome. He looked it up and down. "Emeline, you called this a brick dump. You flattered it. But some day this here Chicago Avenue property will be valuable."

"What's your advice, Mr. Moody?"

"Buy it up fast and cheap. They quoted you $55,-000. Buy it. Now then, let's go around the corner, so you can point out those houses on LaSalle Street."

Standing there in the sooty wind, D.L. prayed that he was doing the right thing. These people had waited so patiently for his advice, his weight behind their project. Now he had given his advice, standing on a street corner, saying buy this, buy that.

He knew that he would not be done with it so easily. He supposed that before long somebody would be trying to call it "Moody's Institute." He said the name over to himself and he liked the sound of it. So many years ago he had walked these streets and dreamed about his name on some tall building—a factory or a warehouse. But a school?

Let them call this school what they wanted to. He knew that he had brought it into being as surely as he had the two in the Connecticut River Valley. Already there was a big place in his heart for the new school and the young men and women who would come to it because they wanted to know more about the Word of God and how to communicate their learning to others.

This had been the city that had let him breathe and be himself and grow. Now he could give something back to it.

D.L. turned and looked into the intense, sharp face of Emeline Dryer. "You satisfied now?" he said lightly. "Looks like you're getting a school at last."

Later that year he recalled the springtime in Chicago and he wrote a letter to a good friend in Scotland. In it he said, "I feel now, if I should go away, the work will go on. I'll always look back on this year as the year I reached the top of the hill."

Chapter Eighteen

DR. ANDREW CLARKE watched him steadily as he put on his black vest and retied his bow tie. The British heart specialist made D.L. uneasy. His fingers fumbled at the buttons. Worst thing about this session was getting his vest buttoned up again, he puffed. But he shouldn't complain about extra pounds. They must be a good sign. Nothing could be wrong with a big healthy ox.

He crossed the room and sat down beside the desk. "Well, I was just thinking that the worse thing about this little session is the bill—and getting back into my vest."

Dr. Clarke tapped his desk top with a nervous finger. He did not look up. "Mr. Moody, I have examined your heart thoroughly. I can come to only one conclusion." The specialist looked directly at D.L. "Your heart has been severely strained."

For a long minute, there was no sound in the room but the rhythmic beating of a clock somewhere on the wall in back of D.L. It seemed to speed up like an overactive heart, ticking so loudly that it blotted out coherent thinking. Then it receded. In the quietness he tried to assimilate what the doctor had told him. Was it true? What would it mean? Slow down? He had never planned on that, had never thought about it.

The three years since he began the Bible Institute in Chicago had been full—his third preaching junket around Great Britain, a tour of the Holy Land, then back again in '92 for more preaching in England and Ireland. Now it was ending in an antiseptic white London office, with a doctor who filled the antiseptic air with germs of gloom.

But D.L. had no intention of slackening the pace established in his twenties. "Stuff and nonsense, doctor," he said. "Big healthy ox like me. I ask you, what in the world did I ever do to make my heart act up?"

"Mr. Moody, how many times a day do you preach?"

D. L. folded his hands over his fat stomach. "Three, most days."

"How many days in the week?" the specialist probed.

"Five days. Why?"

Dr. Andrew Clarke picked up his pen, pulled his files toward him as if he were about to make a notation, then pushed them aside. "Mr. Moody, you are a fool. What have you done to strain your heart? It's more than preaching. It's traveling all night in a coach. Rushing through meals to get to a meeting on time. Shaking hands till midnight. Up to catch a seven o'clock train. You're not a young man. You're fifty-five. Mr. Moody, you're killing yourself."

His folded hands tightened but he tried to sound offhand. "You trying to tell me preaching strains my heart? Hah! Besides, Doc, I always take Saturday off to rest."

"Mr. Moody, this is a serious warning."

D.L. shrugged. "So that's what it is. A warning. Sounds mighty impressive." His momentary tension turned to anger. "Suppose you'll charge accordingly. Cut back, huh?" The Devil himself couldn't whisper anything more malicious. Abruptly, he switched. "Doctor, how hard do you work? How many hours a day? Ten, twelve, sixteen?"

"Why—uh—sixteen or seventeen, rough." The doctor was caught off guard.

"You take a day off?"

"Well, there's a shortage—."

"Sixteen hours, seven days a week." D.L. leaned back in his chair and studied benignly the white wall over the doctor's head.

"Now, Mr. Moody—."

D.L. smiled. "Doc Clarke, you're a bigger fool than I am. You want to know something? Your heart'll give out from overwork before mine."

Later, going along London streets, he chuckled to himself over his last word. But underneath the

146

chuckle, he was fearful. Emma had already sailed for the states. She would not have to know about the doctor's report and she would not be on hand to worry. He would not cut down. But he could not always resist Emma's coaxing. As he walked along the foggy streets, he wondered if this time he could resist his own common sense.

He finished his last meetings in England that fall. In November, 1892, he boarded the German liner "Spree" for home. His son, Will, now 22, had waited to return with him.

As usual, D.L. was seasick as soon as the ship left Liverpool. He was able to push away the warnings of heart trouble, but seasickness conquered him. "Will, son, be kind. Stop eating that—," he moaned and tried to turn over in the bunk— "that pink candy."

Will, his mouth full, looked up from a book. "This? But, Dad, we got about six boxes of it. The London committee brought them on board."

D.L. moaned. "Never want to see candy again. Or the London committee. Never."

Will shrugged and went back to his book. D.L. moaned to himself but the tremorous moan was suddenly obliterated. Outside, there was a walloping crash, like the roar of collapsing roofs in the Chicago fire. After the crash, everything was still. Even the ship's sickening lurch was gone. The engines had stopped.

Will pulled open the cabin door. In the distance, people were running. A man shouted, "She's flooding, sir." A woman screamed. Behind it all was the terrifying silence of the cessation of engines.

"Stay there, Dad. I'm going up on deck."

"Of course, I'll stay here." D.L. swung wobbly legs over the bunk's edge.

Then Will was back, out of breath, panicky. "Dad, get out of bed. We have to get up on deck. Fast."

D.L. eased his big frame over the side of the bunk. He was too sick to be scared. "First time Moody's seen ship's deck out of port," he said bleakly. "Hand me my shoes, son."

Will was already at the cabin door. "Dad, hurry."

When they reached the deck, they saw a crowd showing panic in a hundred ways. There was a woman with a quietly dazed smile, holding half a dozen bright hats and nothing else. Fathers with young wives and small children explained in loud, courageous words what had happened. There was a subtle, but concentrated, edging toward the lifeboats, as if many people thought that they alone knew the boats were there.

But there was no noise. Everyone was listening hopefully for the engines. When the captain appeared, megaphone in hand, there was an indrawing of breath.

In spite of the megaphone, the captain's nervous speech was partly blown out to sea. ". . . accident in engine room. Ship's driving shaft broken . . . punctured outer wall of ship's stern. . . . Three forward bulkheads closed to stop further leakage into the . . ." A woman screamed.

". . . engines rendered useless. These are . . . instructions. Go to *salon*. Wait there until you are signaled on deck. Help in . . . hours. Repeat. Go to . . ."

At ten o'clock that night, they were still in the *salon*. The tension was turning into exhaustion. A few people paced aimlessly. Most talked in low voices. Mirthlessly, D.L. realized that his seasickness was cured. Since the engines stopped, he had forgotten it.

Outside, a rocket whirred. Then a second.

"That ought to get somebody," D.L. remarked to Will.

But Will replied, "Dad, is the floor—does it slant?"

D.L. made his voice calm. "Believe it does, son." The stern of the ship was settling; the bow was pointing the way the rockets had gone.

Three hundred people spent the night in the big drafty room. The ship lurched and rolled. D.L. recalled other sailings and was sure that they must now be almost out of the track of the other big steamers. Who would see their signal?

The next morning—it was Sunday—the ship listed badly. D.L. studied the men and women waking up on the floor. He knew crowds so well. There was an apathy here that might be snapped instantaneously and changed to frenzy. But he could create another mood. He could weave his old magic with some fast-spirited hymns. Then some Scripture to give people hope—no matter what.

The captain granted permission. D.L. braced himself against a pillar, reading from the Bible as calmly as if he were in the North Market Sunday School. People sat up. They turned around so they could watch.

A German man quietly volunteered to translate everything for the passengers who spoke no English. "He will give his angels charge over thee to keep thee in all thy ways."

Then he talked about death. He explained what death was to a Christian. Very simply he told what it was to a man who was not a Christian.

"Now we're going to sing. We'll start off with a few hymns that's got some beat to them. Anybody here know 'There Is Power in the Blood'? Two ladies over there? Good! I do. And my son. That's a quartette. We'll teach the rest. All right, let all the people sing."

When Sunday ended, they were still waiting. Huddled on the *salon* floor, his stubby legs crooked under him, D.L. faced the terrible truth that this might be the last night he would be alive. The ship had been drifting for thirty-six hours. It would not stay afloat much longer.

"God, there's too much to leave. Emma. The children. My schools. God, I'm too much a human being to want to die. Life's been good, because I gave it up to You. So the world could see what You could do—." While the ship lurched and the *salon* filled with the smell of spilled coffee, sick babies, and the sweat of frightened people, he fought back rebellion. At last, weakly, he prayed. "All right, God. Not my will. Thy will be done."

Then he leaned against the pillar. Northfield or Chicago or Heaven? After all, what difference? Still his mind raced to Chicago, to his school and the great World's Fair coming up in '93. Again he prayed. "Now, God, I don't believe in bargaining. But if I see dry land again, I'll forget about slowing down. I'll do the hardest thing I could for You. I'll do what I dreamed about in England. I'll preach at that Chicago World's Fair. If I see dry land again."

He slept for awhile, and then it was three o'clock. "Attention all passengers. All passengers report on deck. Help is sighted."

Everybody started up at once. Sliding along the slanting floor, laughing together, sleepy, he and Will made their way to the deck. The "Lake Huron," an American boat, had sighted the rockets and turned off her course.

150

But exhilaration turned to new fright. The sea was wild. Three times tow lines sailed through the air, fell short, and dangled in foam. Rescue was abandoned.

"Attention, all passengers. We expect to try again in approximately three hours."

"What'll we do now, Dad?" Will asked.

"You heard the captain. Go back and try to sleep."

"If we could only do something—."

"We can. Pray for a calm sea in the morning. Seems like that's all anybody can do now."

The captain's call came at dawn. As he straightened out his aching legs, D. L. knew that prayer was answered. The ship was floating on a smooth sea. On deck he saw the bright sun glittering on gray glass. The tow-line cable had already been secured.

So they started back to Queenstown. As he watched the gray water slide by, he recalled the night. So he had been too much of a human being to want to die. It was true, but something else was also true. The world had *yet* to see what God could do with one man wholly committed to Him. D.L. Moody was going home to the United States and he was not through letting God use him for hard work.

Chapter Nineteen

HIS WONDERFUL CHICAGO had gone mad over night! The World's Fair had arrived—a big, brawling show-off, determined to sweat and shout through the miserably hot summer of '93. Out on a prairieland patch side-show tents, exhibit booths, and flimsy hotels grew overnight. This was the Fair grounds, all dolled up with poster paint, smelling like badly cooked food and set to the tune of band music. A million Chicagoans waited for the United States to come to the show.

D.L. did not like the hoopla but he understood it. The Fair meant a crowd, and there was nothing D.L. understood better than a crowd. The rowdy circus crowd in the Chicago streets did not frighten him. This was the kind of people he wanted to reach with the Gospel, and he was pretty sure he knew how to do it.

"Don't forget the big performance Sunday afternoon, folks. The biggest, most stupendous, most magnificent show you've ever seen. Come one, come all. And get the thrill of your lives. And now folks, step right up, come right in, yes, sirree!" Forepaugh's circus barker wound up his spiel and jumped down from the box. D.L. waited.

"You the manager of this outfit?"

The barker shouldered a coil of rope. "What d'ya want?"

"Sir, you have the finest, biggest tent anywhere in the city." Forepaugh's manager and barker stopped, grinning.

"Do you have a circus here Sunday morning?" D.L. asked.

"What's the matter, fatty. Ain't two shows on Sunday enough for you?"

"I want to make a deal with you," D.L. answered. "I want to rent your tent on Sunday morning."

The manager hoisted the rope and started off. "Suppose you got your own flea-bitten circus. You happen to want to share our facilities."

D.L. walked beside him. "No competition. I want to use your tent for church services."

"That's a hot one."

"I think so. I guess you don't know who I am. I'm D.L. Moody."

This was all a part of strategy, he told the startled circus manager. He was covering the city with meetings wherever the Fair crowd congregated. Had he heard about the meetings in Haymarket Theater? The theater had been full the first night. Nine other city theaters and halls had also been rented for preaching and had been filled regularly. Five tents umbrellaed over the city. Two Gospel wagons toured the streets, handing out free tracts, starting street meetings. What's more, he had brought about forty preachers to the city, some all the way from England. He would not run short on preaching talent. Or on helpers. The students at the new Bible Institute did everything from inquiry room counseling to table waiting.

"Surveying the ground, I think your tent is just about the most popular place in the whole city," D.L. finished. "So I want to borrow it for Sunday meetings."

"Thanks for the compliment," Forepaugh's manager interrupted. "And thanks for the details on how you stage them revivals. But I ain't interested."

"But, sir—."

"I like just one thing. Do you pay?"

"Of course."

"All right. If you got my kind of money, maybe we can talk a deal."

Later D.L. went into the afternoon show to study the tent. It seated ten thousand. From overhead dangled ropes and trapezes. It smelled of animals. He sniffed. Elephants. But it seated ten thousand.

153

As he left the tent, he saw the manager talk to a roustabout. They were laughing. D.L. knew what they thought. "Who'll come to church in a circus tent?"

When he saw the signs the next day, he was more sure. They read: "Ha! Ha! Ha! Three big shows. Moody in the morning. Forepaugh Circus in the afternoon and evening."

But it was no show. It was a preaching service. First they sang to forget the elephant smells and the pink crepe paper. Then D.L. preached. On the first Sunday, Forepaugh's tent was full. The second Sunday was the same.

When D.L. heard what happened on Sunday afternoon in the tent, he could imagine the incredulous fury of the circus manager.

"All that guy Moody's fault," he had probably raged.

"How come?"

"I dunno. All I know is he packed the tent this morning. Now this afternoon, it ain't even half full."

D.L. felt a little sorry for the manager. He had wanted to beat the Fair. But beating it was getting a crowd to hear the Gospel. He had not rented the tent to stop the show. He was not prepared for the manager's growls when next they met.

"Moody, when competition's got me beat, I'll face it. Your Sunday show's bigger'n mine. I'm calling m ne quits."

D.L. tried to keep the encounter light. "Fat man on Sunday morning is a better show than the fat men in Forepaugh's side show, huh?"

"You're a show all right," the manager said. "I seen them for a quarter of a century and I never thought I'd see a tent packed with what oughta be a circus crowd singing hymns and hearing hellfire preached at them." He grabbed D.L. by the lapel. "Listen, Moody, I got a proposition to make to you. How about joining my show?"

"What?"

"I know a good thing when I see one. When we go on the road next, I been thinking of turning Sunday over to religion. No, you ain't converted me yet, Moody. Not by a long shot. But suppose you and me work together or maybe one of your evangelizing sidekicks. If you can't beat 'em, join 'em."

D.L. explained that this was out of the question. But he was flattered. "If you can't beat 'em, join 'em, eh? Well, as one World's Fair showman to another, thanks for the compliment."

He had kept the promise he made to God on the listing ship. He had done the hardest thing he could. He had taken Gospel preaching to the Chicago World's Fair and, in his own way, he had "beaten the Fair." Walking away from the tent, he knew something else too. He had done it because he had done it all for God, not in his own strength.

In the fall, the Fair closed. D.L. went right on— operating his three schools, overseeing the Chicago Avenue Church, and preaching. In 1894, he held revivals in Washington, Toronto, Birmingham, Scranton, and half a dozen other cities in the United States and Canada.

In 1895, he preached in Boston, Worcester, New York City, and Philadelphia. In 1897 was a whirlwind. He hopped from Cincinnati to Chicago again and on to Winnipeg. Occasionally, waiting for a train, he remembered the British heart specialist's antiseptic white office. But he tried to forget it.

In 1898, there was war again, the Spanish-American War. D.L. was drafted to head up the YMCA's troop evangelism. Tackling his administrative desk duties, he wistfully remembered the front lines at Shiloh and Murfreesboro, more than thirty years before.

Then it was 1899. He traveled to California, preaching in Santa Barbara, Los Angeles, Phoenix, San Diego. After that he came back to Northfield. Emma was at Northfield with Will and his family, and young Emma and her husband, Percy Arthur Fitt, D.L.'s right-hand worker since they met in Dublin seven years before.

Arriving at the farm, D.L. had a job for his son-in-law. "That's right. I said Kansas City, Fitt. They've invited me. I want you to go out and get the lay of the land."

But his son-in-law was unenthusiastic. "Dad, you need a rest—until after the first of the year, anyway. Stay in Northfield through Christmas."

"Fitt, maybe you didn't hear me straight. Kansas City folks have invited me to preach to them." Probably the truth was that he wanted his wife to stay at home with the new baby.

"Dad, D.L. Moody isn't quite the same D.L. Moody he was when he preached in the Hippodrome. That was more than twenty-five years ago."

"Strong as ever. Only sixty-two."

"Old enough to mind the doctor."

"Forget the doctors." This young fellow was trying to say he was not the same man. Maybe so. He might grant it. But God was the same God. He spoke sharply to Fitt. "I expect you better get along over to your house. Emma will want to start your packing if you're to leave by the weekend."

His son-in-law went to Kansas City. When he returned to report on arrangements, D.L. knew that something was wrong.

"It's the hall," Fitt told him as they ate breakfast together the first morning.

"Too small?"

"Too big!"

"Too big!" D.L. spiked a third pancake. "Ain't seen a hall yet that's too big."

"They say this is. Too big for Kansas anyway. I found out that the only man that ever filled it was William Jennings Bryan and he nearly wore himself out." Fitt turned to Emma, fluttering nearby with the syrup. "Mother, I don't like to see Dad try this. I think this hall is a killer."

For ten minutes, they coaxed and scolded him. When they were through, he said, "Whether I fill that hall out there or not, that's not the important thing. Whether I go to Kansas City and preach, like I think God wants me to, that's what counts. I am going. Forget my heart. Forget the doctor. Forget my age. I'm going to Kansas City."

He left Northfield early in November. The train ride tired him. Even stopping over in Philadelphia to see his good friend John Wanamaker did not brush away the fatigue. In Kansas City he felt—even before his first meeting was over—that he was pushing more than usual. He felt as if he were rolling a heavy ball uphill. But the crowds were there.

On the fifth night he clutched the pulpit and shouted, "It's a great thing to see a full house. God bless you all. They told me I couldn't fill the Kansas City auditorium, and I told them they were right. I couldn't. But God could. They said I couldn't reach you folks in the last balcony, and I said I wouldn't worry about it, God could. It's the fifth night, and

157

you're all still here. The house is full again tonight. God bless you all!"

Two weeks later it was another story. Brought home from Kansas City in a special Pullman, he was nursed by Emma in the upper bedroom of the North-field farm. On the afternoon of December 22, 1899, he said, "God is calling me. There's no pain. No valley. This is glorious." The family were all there, waiting.

Half an hour later, he shook his big frame. "Get me over to a chair. I think God'll do a miracle after all."

But he was wrong. The miracle had already been done. And it had been done because the country boy from Northfield decided that he no longer wanted to make something of himself merely for himself, because he turned his energy, his lack of education, his strange gift of persuading people, and his business skill over to God. The miracle had been done when the ex-shoe salesman and free-lance religious worker took to heart the words, *The world has yet to see what God can do with one man wholly committed to Him.*

Moody Press, a ministry of the Moody Bible Institute, is designed for education, evangelization and edification. If we may assist you in knowing more about Christ and the Christian life, please write us without obligation to: Moody Press, c/o MLM, Chicago, Illinois 60610.

Bibliography
used for research

BOYD, ROBERT. *The Wonderful Career of Moody and Sankey* in Great Britain and America. N. Y.: H. S. Goodspeed & Co., 1875.

BRADFORD, GAMALIEL. *D.L. Moody, Worker in Souls.* N. Y.: Geo. H. Doran, 1927.

CHAPMAN, J. WILBUR. *Life and Work of Dwight L. Moody.* N. Y., Phila. etc., 1900 various pub.

DANIELS, W. H. *D. L. Moody and His Work.* N. Y.: American Pub. Co., 1875.

DAY, RICHARD. *Bush Aglow.* Phila.: Judson Press, 1936.

ERDMAN, CHARLES. *Dwight Moody, His Message for Today.* Westwood, N. J.: F. H. Revell Co., 1928.

FITT, A. P. *Moody Still Lives.* Westwood, N. J.: Revell, 1936.

POWELL, EMMA. *Heavenly Destiny.* Chicago: Moody Press, 1943.

MOODY, PAUL. *My Father.* Boston: Little, Brown & Co., 1938.

MOODY, WILLIAM. *The Life of Dwight L. Moody,* Westwood, N. J.: Revell, 1900.

DUFFUS, R. L. *"The Hound of Heaven" in American Mercury,* April, 1925.